1

Oh, Darling! : Choices and Struggle in the Age of Sputnik,
the Vietnam War & the New Millennium
By James Jones

A15 Publishing
5219 Monticello Avenue #5037
Williamsburg, VA 23188-9998

WWW.A15Publishing.com

Introduction

I was drafted into the U.S. Army as a 19-year-old in 1966. After basic training at Fort Benning, Ga., I completed light weapons infantry training at Fort Ord, Calif., and earned a commission as a second lieutenant through Signal OCS at Fort Gordon.

"Oh, Darling" is a nonfiction book about my time as a soldier serving in Vietnam, initially as an assistant battalion operations officer, later as a company commander, and finally as a brigade staff officer deeply involved in "Vietnamization" of the war. It is also about how a beautiful Vietnamese woman who worked for the U.S. Army changed my life forever. We worked more than a year to win government approval to get married, including traveling thousands of miles between two continents. What could go wrong?

"Oh, Darling" combines personal experience with history, and popular culture. The book is about struggle, perseverance, and the power of love. Nearly 40 years after the war, we returned to Vietnam together to the places we knew in our youth.

"Oh, Darling" draws on my 9 1/2 years of active duty, including 33 months in Vietnam, and my work as a newspaper editor/writer from 1977-through present day. Along the way, there have been brushes with notables, like LBJ, John Glenn, and Yoko Ono.

In this life, we often stumble, but occasionally we soar, too.

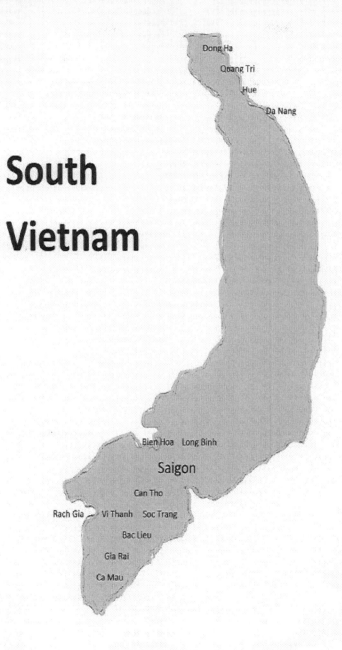

South

Vietnam

Dong Ha
Quang Tri
Hue
Da Nang

Bien Hoa   Long Binh

Saigon

Can Tho
Rach Gia   Vi Thanh   Soc Trang
Bac Lieu
Gia Rai
Ca Mau

Preface

After many years telling the stories of others, I found that writing about my Vietnam War experiences proved to be more difficult than I ever imagined. It was a challenge getting inside my head to confront my shortcomings — there are many — and to write without overly burnishing any achievements. I wrestled with how to write sensitively about deeply personal relationships. Because at its center, "Oh, Darling" is an incongruous love story.

It seemed to me that if I was to tell the story, that I needed to share something of the years before the war, and after, as painful as those years occasionally were. Inevitably, "Oh, Darling" is part history, part memoir, and part musing on the culture of our times.

It's a story about choices, and about struggle.

Millions of Americans and Vietnamese were caught up in the tragedy of a war that seemed to be without end, and which continues to have profound consequences. This is one of those stories, written in fits and starts over a five-year period. Invaluable to this project was the insight and suggestions from friends and family about content, story flow, organization, and whether it all makes sense. They responded with patience and wisdom, and hopefully helped me craft something insightful and coherent.

For their reading and suggestions, a great debt is owed to journalists George Meyer, Gary Taylor, Jennifer Rich, Vin Mannix, Art Durshimer, and Larry Leech.

Equally important were the comments of family members Christine Dieu Jones, Sandra Lee Spurlock, and Verona Wiggins, and of my long-time friend Bernice Christiansen, who has known me since my first newspaper job in 1977.

Special thanks to Col. Earl L. Tingle Jr., an Officer Candidate School classmate, for bringing his critical eye and experience as a career officer to this task.

Thanks also to Fred Freund, who befriended me in Vietnam and remained a friend and mentor for life. Fred's family allowed me to excerpt his unfinished memoir.

Thanks also to Thomas D. Alcorn who allowed me unfettered access to 14 years of material written for the New Smyrna Beach Observer.

Some of the subject matter on our return to Vietnam previously appeared in the Bradenton Herald, and has been rewritten, updated and adapted for this book.

There is an element of survivor's guilt associated with my experiences in Vietnam. It is to the more than 58,000 Americans who died in the war that this book is dedicated.

Inspiration? That's all Kim. "Oh, Darling" is written for her. Stubborn thing, love. It is resolute, knowing only what is, and what must be.

Table of contents

Preface
Place map
Introduction
Chapters

1 – Glimmers

Blanche Jones and her oldest son, Leslie. In all, she gave birth to 12 children.

SOUTH BOSTON, Va.

My grandparents were as tired and broken down as their farmhouse. Why shouldn't they have been? They were old. They had been worn down by a life of hard work, tragedy and disappointment. The house dated to the Civil War and had seen better days. The floors bounced and creaked whenever someone walked from one room to another. Rubbery, sagging stairs led upstairs to two bedrooms, where the walls merged toward the center of the tongue-and-groove ceiling. Everything about the house sagged toward the middle, including the large beds upstairs with iron headboards. Even so, my father and his nine surviving siblings seemed to relish returning there for family reunions. They had been conceived, born, and raised on the farm. Several had gone on to work in area textile mills. Or like my father, had become mechanics. None had gone on to great prosperity. No matter, at the reunions they enjoyed the country cooking — the fried chicken, the potato salad, and a baker's dozen of pies spread out on wooden tables outside. And they enjoyed cutting loose with practical jokes and other shenanigans.

The brothers seemed drawn to whatever car was parked in the gravel driveway with its hood up. They would stand under the shade of a walnut tree, bottle of beer in hand, trying to figure out why the car would not crank. "It's a Ford," my uncle Robert would say, repeating an age-old joke. "Fix or repair daily." That sparked a never-ending debate about whether Ford or Chevy was better. The women would be in the kitchen, shelling peas, cooking, talking, and probably expressing disappointment with their men.

At night, the yard and hills would be alive with lightning bugs, as children played hide and seek.

My grandparents' farmhouse in South Boston, Va., was just two counties away from Appomattox Courthouse.

Those are some of my memories of life at the humble farmhouse outside South Boston, Va., from the late 1940s into the early 1960s. I was born at home on Chalmers Street in downtown South Boston in 1946 but spent a lot of time at my grandparents' farm. The scent of harsh soap and sweat seemed to linger in the air at the farmhouse. Distant markers of those who came before.

Ghostly mules and spectral men, plowing the hard, red clay on hot summer days, geeing and hawing. Yes, there seemed to be spirits who haunted the farm though they managed to remain out of sight. I saw that farming was back-breaking work. Pulling Jimson

2

weed. Topping suckers from tobacco plants. Milking cows. Shoveling manure. Slopping hogs.

Family members gathered under kerosene lamps at night to talk about what they had done that day. About townspeople who might have gotten married. And, always, who had died.

There was a sense of loss which could not be seen, only felt: a baby girl named Gladys Virginia Jones who died at five-days-old, and who was buried next to her older sister Mary.

Mary had mysteriously died at 19, perhaps at the hand of her husband. The family always had their suspicions. A son, George, a 20-year-old infantryman, died in Italy in 1944, fighting Nazis.

My grandmother lost her father early. He stepped on a rusty nail and died of lockjaw — tetanus — while he was in his 30s. Life was hard in those days.

The rambling two-story farmhouse sat on a hill overlooking an apple orchard, a smokehouse, and a tobacco curing barn. A creek meandered through the property, a favorite skinny-dipping spot for children. My grandmother made clothes for the family from cloth flour bags. She canned tomatoes, okra, and apples in Mason jars and stored them under the house in a stone cellar.

When my father was growing up, he fetched water from the spring in the valley and lugged it up the hill. Later, the family dug a well in the front yard, and winched it up by the bucket. This was progress, but still there was no running water in the house. Family members bathed in enamel wash basins with water heated on the stove. Into the 1960s, there was a two-seater outhouse in the back yard.

Down a path from the house was a rickety, unpainted wooden barn. Dust from the hay seemed to dance in the sunlight that streamed through gaps in the wall slats. I have a memory of my grandfather, wearing black rubber boots, khaki pants, and a white shirt, herding his cows out of the barn to the pasture in the morning, and bringing them home in the evening. He milked by hand, and loaded galvanized cans of milk into his battered pickup truck for the drive to the Carnation dairy a few miles away.

In her later years, my grandmother was a little eccentric. She would yell at the television set when pro wrestling aired, convinced that the carnage meted out by Gorgeous George was real. No one was allowed into my grandmother's parlor, which she kept locked. It provided an endless source of fascination for children who peeped through the keyhole, trying to see what she kept there.

My grandfather was sweet and kind, totally under the control of my grandmother. Both were wonderful to their grandchildren, leading me to the misconception that all old folks were kindly and wise.

Into the early 1950s, the home had no electricity. Farm life had changed little in the last 100 years, except for the plowing. There was a Ford tractor under a pole barn, and mules and horses in the pasture. After my grandparents died, the farmhouse passed out of the family. The house was torn down and the property sold. But while it stood, the old house would send my imagination racing with thoughts of long-dead soldiers in blue or gray marching to battle. After all, this was Halifax County, just two counties away from Appomattox Courthouse where Robert E. Lee surrendered to U.S. Grant in 1865.

My imagination also took me to the future, and I endlessly asked myself, "What will I become?" Never in my wildest dreams did I imagine wearing an Army uniform, or going to war in a place called Vietnam. Not that I had ever heard of Vietnam.

Nor that there was a little girl named Kim living there who would one day change my life.

2 - Blood

There were the wispiest of stories I heard during my childhood of ancestors who fought in the Civil War. They all wore Confederate gray. It was tantalizing trying to imagine what they had done, but there were no specifics. None.

Decades later, I delved into family genealogy, and found that my ancestors were much like their descendants. Common folk. No plantation owners, or notable leaders. Nor were there captains of industry. My Civil War ancestors were the smallest of bit players on the wrong side of history.

Whitt Cassada

Players in the original sin, slavery, that blighted this country from its founding. Uncredited players in an existential crisis, the worst in U.S. history. Beyond a few basic facts, it is impossible to know what was in their hearts, or to measure their character. My grandmother, Sallie Blanche Jones, talked about the past simply. The way country people talked about the tobacco crop or hams curing in the smoke house.

Blanche's grandfather, Whitt Cassada, served with Stonewall Jackson during the Civil War. He was wounded in the leg charging a battery of union artillery during the first battle of Kernstown on March 23, 1862, near Winchester, Virginia. Two of Whitt's brothers died in the war. Pvt. Shadrack Cassada died on July 7, 1862, of wounds after the Seven Days Battle. Lt. John J. Cassada died from his wounds after being shot at Drewrys Bluff, Va., in 1864. Shortly after John Cassada was killed, Whitt deserted and went home. Some speculate that it was to help take care of his family. Whitt later returned to active duty and rejoined the fight. Otherwise, he might have been shot or hanged, however they dealt with deserters back then. It is a little disturbing to learn that an ancestor had been a deserter. But facts are facts.

On my mother's side of the family, her great-grandfathers, Duncan Johnson and Seaborn Griffin, were members of the Florida state militia during the Civil War. Seaborn was wounded in the thigh during a skirmish with federal troops who landed at St. Andrews, Fla. The union troops were there to disrupt Confederate salt works. And there were many more, dirt farmers and sharecroppers mostly, who were swept up in something that even now is difficult to comprehend. Yes, the war would have seemed very unpleasant and near for my grandparents, and great-grandparents.

During World War II, the "good war," my family again had skin in the game. George Cassada Jones, one of my father's younger brothers, and their first cousin, Haywood Lellon Southard, died within six weeks of each other in the European Theatre.

My father was a mechanic serving with the Third Army, while his brother Presley was a medic in England. George was an infantryman with the 363rd Infantry Regiment, 91st Infantry Division, fighting its way through Italy.

The brothers stayed in contact by letter, and then one day the letters from George stopped. He had been killed in action in Italy on Aug. 17, 1944. Shot by a sniper while on guard duty.

George is buried in the Florence American Cemetery in Italy.

George Cassada Jones

What more can we say about George? He was 20, and never married. His Army portrait shows a jaunty young man smiling into the camera. His crisp khaki uniform is perfect, reflecting his pride in serving his country. He stood 5 foot 10 and weighed 150 pounds.

6

He had blue eyes and blond hair. He worked at the Halifax Cotton Mill before the war. His draft registration indicates that his work experience was as a farm hand. Family members would later say he was a free spirit and would not shrink from taking chances. Like the other World War II draftees, his enlistment was for the duration of the war or other emergency, plus six months, subject to the discretion of the president or otherwise according to law.

Haywood Lellon Southard

His Purple Heart has come down through the family to me. When I first held his medal, it put a lump in my throat as I reflected on his sacrifice and the full life that he was unable to have. There should be so much more to say about George. George's death followed that of his first cousin, Haywood, 19, on July 5, 1944, in France. Haywood died of wounds he suffered in battle, just a month after the Allied invasion of Normandy. Haywood was the son of my grandmother's sister, Pearlie. It's hard to imagine the family's grief at losing two sons six weeks apart. For those battle deaths, Blanche never forgave the Germans.

Later, my father's youngest brother, Robert, served in Korea, and was awarded the Combat Infantry Badge. Also serving in World War II was my mom's older brother, Marion, who went into the Navy at age 17. All three of my mother's younger brothers served in the Marine Reserve during the 1950s and early 1960s. The youngest brother retired as a chief warrant officer with the Florida National Guard.

Chandler Monroe Johnson, my maternal grandfather, is shown in his World War I uniform.

Perhaps the Johnson boys were just following the example of their father, Chandler Johnson, who served in the Army during World War I. All of his service was stateside, just a few months before the Armistice was declared. Ever proud of his time in uniform, Chandler later served as a civilian air raid warden in St. Augustine during World War II.

Yes, there was a long family history of serving in the armed forces. Maybe the Civil War seemed like ancient history, but it seemed close, too.

And World War II? Well, that was yesterday.

3 — Fresh from the farm

My grandfather, Alfred Jefferson Jones, shows off his work horses.

My parents knew all about the school of hard knocks. They shared a farm background and a less-than-stellar history as scholars. Both were school dropouts. Thelma left school after the eighth grade. My dad dropped out after the seventh grade in the midst of the Great Depression and went to work for a state road crew. His parents begged him to stay in school because he was a good student. They said they would even try to help pay his way through college. But my dad was stubborn. He could earn as much as a grown man carrying water for a road construction crew and doing other menial jobs. It was a decision he lived to regret. His family didn't need the money. The Great Depression hardly touched his family. They grew the food they needed on the farm; corn, beans, wheat, and tomatoes. They raised and slaughtered hogs and cattle for meat. Tobacco was the money crop. My grandfather, Alfred Jefferson Jones, had a job with the Virginia road department, and on Sundays would preach fiery old-time religion from the pulpit as a lay preacher. As my father grew into a young man, he gave farming a try, but quit after earning just enough from his crop to buy a new set of overalls. Farming was, and is, a risky business. He went to work at Slayton's Garage in Halifax, and proved an apt student, learning all aspects of the trade,

Alfred Jefferson Jones, in his Sunday best.

My dad, James A. Jones Sr., before he was drafted into the Army.

including teardown and repair of engines and transmissions. He reputedly became the highest paid mechanic in Halifax County. Those skills served him well when he was drafted into the Army on May 6, 1941, seven months before the Japanese bombed Pearl Harbor. The Army promoted him from private in basic training to tech sergeant within four months. "I could do in a day what they were teaching the other soldiers to do in a week," he said. He learned to repair and rebuild all kinds of military vehicles, everything from tanks and half-tracks to Jeeps. Initially, he was stationed close to home at Fort Lee, Va., and Aberdeen Providing Grounds in Maryland.

That changed with Pearl Harbor. He was in a stateside movie theater at the time of the attack. Someone entered the auditorium and shouted that all military personnel should immediately report to post.

Eventually, he was assigned to Saint Augustine, Fla., living in an Army tent city on Francis Field, next door to Ketterlinus High School. From there it was a short walk downtown to Alexander's Restaurant, where Thelma Louise Johnson, my future mother, was working as a teenager. My father stopped in there a few times and struck up a friendship with Thelma. That would have been in early 1944, the same year that Thelma's father died of a heart attack. "I just liked her," my father said of his attraction to slender, dark-eyed Thelma.

*My mother, Thelma, at left, with her father, Chandler, and baby
sister Verona, in St. Augustine during World War II.*

Her family had been devastated by the Great Depression. My great-grandfather, Thomas Jefferson Butler, tried to kill himself after his farming operation near Hastings, Fla., failed in the economic collapse. But he succeeded only in crippling himself. He would live another three decades and get around on crutches. When the family farm failed, Chandler Monroe Johnson, my mother's father, who had been renowned for the straight furrows he plowed, accepted any job he could find, and rode his bicycle to work. He worked in a boat yard in St. Augustine, and as a school custodian. No one knew how sick he was. He died at 48,

Chandler and Bertha Johnson with their youngest child,
Jimmy, in 1943. Chandler had a year left to live, and
Bertha's last pregnancy nearly killed her.

leaving my grandmother with five children to raise from their home at 36 St. George Street in Saint Augustine. A sixth child, her oldest, Marion, was a teenager serving in the U.S. Navy. From that point, my grandmother Bertha's life was an object lesson in survival and love of her children. Asked about the good old days, she had an answer that offered all the insight anyone would need. "What was so good about them? You worked hard from the time you got up in the morning until you went to bed at night," she said. My grandmother used to take the taxi home after shopping at the grocery because she didn't have a car.

One time my mother's youngest brother, Jimmy, got a little too curious about what was in the brown paper sacks, and dropped and broke the eggs. He had been raised to tell the truth, and immediately volunteered with what he had done. When he did, he got a slap in the face, but not too hard I'm sure. "But you always told me to tell the truth," he gasped.

"I didn't slap you for telling the truth. I slapped you for being stupid," my grandmother said.

St. Augustine would be a way station for my father. He was reassigned to Miami, and then shipped to England via New York City on the Queen Mary, a luxury liner that had been converted for use as a troop transport ship. He was stationed in Liverpool, England, long enough to have a girlfriend, Phyllis, from West Darby. It was a serious relationship and my dad thought they might even marry. After D-Day, my father and hundreds of thousands of others joined Allied invasion forces in France.

My dad served with Gen. George Patton's Third Army during World War II. For the better part of a year, he was close to or at the front — steel pot-wearing close — in the mud and the snow, moving among the dead, rotting bodies often piled up roadside.

There were many close calls, including having the windshield shot out of his Jeep while inspecting battle damage. His feet froze during the Battle of the Bulge, leading to a lifetime of medical problems. Before it was over, his European service had taken him to England, Scotland, Wales, France, Luxembourg, Belgium, Czechoslovakia, and Germany.

When the war in Europe ended, my dad was alerted to prepare to be shipped to the Pacific Theater to join the fight against the Japanese. After all he had been though in Europe, he thought he could not survive a second war in the Pacific. Truman's dropping of the atomic bomb on Japan abruptly brought that war to an end, and my father began hoping for a return to civilian life and starting a family. He got a pass to England to visit Phyllis in Liverpool and learned she had married another soldier.

Strangely, my grandmother Blanche and my father's old girlfriend Phyllis continued to exchange letters for decades after the war.

My father was discharged from the Army on Nov. 12, 1945. He was 29. He drove to Florida with $600 that he had saved, and proposed to Thelma. "We were both ready," he later said. They spent their honeymoon and money in Florida, and moved, flat broke, to South Boston. He returned to his old job at Slayton's Garage. A year later, I was born, followed 12 months later by my sister Phyllis — named after my dad's English girlfriend. Our sister Sandra arrived in 1951.

The young couple had high hopes for a better life. After all, they came from hard-working families who made their own clothes and wasted nothing.

Marriage would offer my parents the emotional support and affection they craved, and their hard work would open the door to the American dream. Or so they thought.

James A. Jones Sr., center, during World War II.

4 — Cars, beer and lost love

The alert little guy in blue jeans and plaid shirt, and slicked-down brown hair, second from left, is me. The photo was taken before my parent's divorce. My grandmother Bertha is at left. My father is in the brown suit, and my mother is second from right with my Aunt Margaret. My sister Phyllis is the little girl.
Photo courtesy of Charles Milton Johnson

"We were great lovers," my dad once said of the early years of the marriage. But I knew nothing of that. My early memories in South Boston included trying to climb the side of a pantry when I was about four. My mother had placed a plate of fresh-baked biscuits there to keep them out of my reach. When she went outside to hang clothes to dry, I climbed up to grab a biscuit and pulled the pantry over. The glass door broke over my head. Every dish, cup, and glass in the house shattered. I don't remember feeling any pain, but I do remember the sound of the crash, and blood turning my vision red as my terrified mother rushed back into the house. The jagged glass had sliced off a piece of my scalp. A doctor stitched me up, bandaged my head, and sent me home. I saw my father squatting on the floor, picking up shards of glass scattered across the linoleum.

As I grew older, I carefully combed my hair to conceal a quarter-sized scar, a permanent reminder of my accident. I would not call my boyhood

15

dull and traumatic. Those are mutually exclusive terms. There were elements of both. Those years were not idyllic, although there were idyllic moments. Why should the world be any different for me, than for most of the human race, born without pedigree, privilege or position?

Cars, beer and lost love are at the root of country music. They make for a good song. Over-simplified for sure, but that could have been the theme song of my parents' failed marriage.

My dad with my sister Phyllis and me.

Arthritis crippled my father in the winter, while he was still in his 30s. He had frequent infections in the legs, a carryover from having his feet frozen during World War II. Those infections would send red streaks running up his leg, forcing him into the hospital several times over the years.

Finally, he found it impossible to work in the drafty garage at Slayton's in Halifax, Va., during the winter. The doctor recommended the family move to a warmer climate. My parents packed us into an old Ford, a 1940 model, and in 1952 moved us to St. Augustine, Fla., my mother's hometown. They bought a little house for $3,200 on one acre about a mile south of St. Augustine. The house had two tiny bedrooms, each just large enough to hold a bed and maybe a small dresser. In the living room was a kerosene lamp that had been wired for electricity, hanging from the ceiling. There was a basic fireplace, just an opening in the concrete blocks that fed into the chimney. My dad bricked up the fireplace and installed a gas heater. It was the only heat in the house in winter.

Out back was a one-car shed made of rough, unpainted pine. Most of the homestead was covered in palmettos and pine trees. In the hot Florida weather, my father found he could work again. He took off his shirt

16

waded into the scrub and cleared the property with a grubbing hoe over the next few months.

Thelma, about the time of the breakup.

The house sat on Highland Avenue, a narrow shell road running through the blue-collar neighborhood. The neighbor across the street drove a trash truck, and the fellow next door was a printer. Another neighbor was a mechanic, like my father.

My father found work at the St. Augustine City Garage, where he repaired and serviced police cars, street sweepers and garbage trucks. My mother worked as a waitress at the Blue Bay Café, down on the St. Augustine waterfront.

My parents had become friends with another couple down the street. There was a lot of drinking and partying. In 1956, my mother and father split up. The parting was traumatic. My father tearfully pleaded with my mother not to leave him. My sisters, Phyllis, and Sandra, and I were in tears, too, when we learned one night during a car ride that they were divorcing. Asked who we wanted to live with, we couldn't choose; the choice was too difficult. I was 9 years old, Phyllis was 8, and Sandi was 4. My mother wanted a better life, and no matter how hard she and my father worked, it wasn't happening. "I am getting out of this mud hole," I remember her telling my father, breaking his heart as she left. My mother moved out of town with the new man in her life, a TV repairman. My father kept custody of us and for the next few years he did the best he could. He took us to the beach, and to the St. Johns River where we swam and dug clams with our toes, in a desperate attempt to reintroduce some fun back into our lives. He hired several older women to keep house. One was a great-aunt, who turned out to like sherry too much. She would transform from a cultured lady who talked about Chopin and Valentino into a mean drunk. Another housekeeper was a kindly lady, who we called Aunt Dale. She kept a tidy house and made wonderful bread pudding. My dad fired the drunken aunt, and Aunt Dale died.

We struggled, the house was a mess, and I failed a grade. When there was no housekeeper, my dad would cook potato soup seven days a week, or so it seemed. Maybe it was the Irish in him.

After the divorce, we were cut off from the rest of the family. We saw no one from my mother's side of the family unless we went to my Grandmother Johnson's. We didn't see family from my dad's side of the family either. Most of them were hundreds of miles away in Virginia and North Carolina.

The family gardener and chicken wrangler gets acquainted with a little hard work.

In 1959, my father married a woman named Margie, who worked across the street from the city garage as a supermarket cashier. Margie had three children, all younger than my sisters and me; Nancy, Kathy and Tony. In 1961 Margie and my dad had a daughter, Carolyn, and the family was complete. It was about then that my father decided we needed to have a home garden. My job was to dig up a quarter-acre plot with a shovel, break up the clods, level it and weed it. It was hard work, and I hated it. But I did it. We grew corn, onions, watermelons, tomatoes, eggplant and okra. Later we had a flock of chickens which gave us eggs and meat. My dad gave me another job: chicken wrangler. Part of the job was occasionally slaughtering a chicken. Which I did with a hatchet, taking

18

off their heads. I didn't like killing chickens. I didn't like dipping the carcasses in boiling water, plucking the feathers or gutting the birds. It turned my stomach. I couldn't eat chicken for years afterward.

The house was no longer a mess, but now it was over-crowded and there was conflict between my sisters, Phyllis and Sandi, and Margie. It is a hard job being a stepmother. And it can be even harder being a stepchild. My mother, regretting the decision to leave us behind, fought to get us back. One night she came to the house. There were words and my father pushed her out of the house. In a fury, my mother swung her pocketbook, knocking out the jalousie windows in the front door. My mother might have left empty handed that night, but eventually Sandi and later Phyllis came to her of their own accord.

After they became teens, first Sandi, and then Phyllis, left St. Augustine and moved to Jacksonville to live with our mother. A next-door neighbor acted as the conduit to help get the girls from Saint Augustine to Jacksonville. Phyllis' stay in Jacksonville was short, however, because she couldn't stand the fighting between my mother and the new man in her life.

Although the grievances between stepmother and stepchildren were real, it needs to be said that there came to be a real bond of love and affection between the seven children that persists to this day. There is a photo of little sister, Kathy, riding on my back when she was about three, pretending to smoke a giant cigar. The joy that photo captures is unmistakable.

It was often a rowdy, fun house. On one occasion, Nancy, two years older than Kathy, was jumping off a wood pile in the back yard. It was all fun until she fell the wrong way and broke her arm. I'll never forget her laughter turning to shock and horror as she looked at her forearm, and saw it bent 90 degrees. My dad rushed home from work, placed Nancy's arm on a pillow, and drove her to the hospital. There was no 9-1-1 in Saint Augustine in the early 1960s.

When Phyllis and Sandi moved out, it just made me more determined to stay the course: to wrangle chickens, to dig the garden, to cut the grass, and to help my dad with his home mechanic projects. I learned to tolerate the drama in the house. No matter what happened, I wasn't going anywhere. Not for a while at least.

I found peace in the woods, and as a boy came to love fishing and oystering. That, and my love of running, gave me the outlets I needed.

5 - Changes

Growing up, my best friend and I always seemed to be playing some version of shoot-'em-up, either Americans vs. Germans, or cowboys and Indians in the woods behind my house. We tested our strength and quickness by wrestling in the pine straw or punching each other in the arm to see who could raise the biggest knot and make the other cry uncle first. I envied the tranquility in his house, which had not been traumatized by divorce. His mother would prepare us a lunch of grilled cheese sandwiches and tomato soup, served with a glass of cold sweet tea. When we got old enough to drive, we would go oystering on cold blustery days in the sloughs north of Marineland. More than once, we returned to the car with a load of oysters, our lips blue, our teeth chattering, and our fingers too numb to open the car.

We went fishing in little creeks in the woods, and on the ocean jetties near Saint Augustine. More than once, we were nearly swept away by waves pounding the big rocks, losing our tackle box and bucket of fish. It was a thing of beauty when we landed a sea trout, or hooked a big tarpon, only to see it roll out of the water and effortlessly snap our line. Skinned knees and elbows were just part of the adventure. I can still recall the warmth of the the sun when it came out from behind a cloud on a cold day to warm us after being soaked in sea water. The incredible, raw beauty of the Atlantic Ocean, the woods, and streams were ours to enjoy.

Immersed in the natural world, there was no stress, and no worry. We thought our Huckleberry Finn life would last forever.

We were wrong.

***

At St. Augustine High School, I was an indifferent, lazy student. There were a few things I did well. I could draw and thought that maybe someday I would be an artist. I liked history but didn't enjoy diagramming sentences in English class. I never took an advanced math class. When I studied, I made good grades. When I didn't, I hoped for the best. During one of my intermittent study spurts, I astonished my teacher, Mr. Bruce Bishop, when he called on me several times in civics class with questions, and I answered correctly. "Darn, Jones has turned into a brain," Bishop told the class.

Running was my other talent. The love of running required me to study enough to maintain my eligibility to stay on the track team. I tried the mile run, and then the quarter mile dash, before finally settling on the half mile run. In my senior year, I was the best half miler in Saint Augustine, and after three years on the track team, finally earned a letter.

***

You could hear my great-grandmother, Maggie Butler, coming before you saw her. She clomped around in the high-top shoes that elderly women favored in the 1950s, and she wheezed. Granny had seen and experienced a lot in her life, and the family held her in awe, affection and respect. She was formidable in her strength and wisdom. In 1957, when the Soviet Union launched Sputnik into orbit around the earth, Granny proclaimed that the end of the world was near. When Granny put down her dress making or the little red-and-brown monkeys that she sewed from socks, we all listened. After all, she was born in 1884, so that would have made her an impossibly old 73 in 1957. "The apocalypse is coming," she said. I was 10 years old then, and fearful for a while that Granny was correct. After a few weeks, the anxiety subsided, and our attention turned to the United States' initial clumsy efforts to launch its first satellite.

A few years later, we were regulars at McDowell Baptist Church, where Brother Frederick preached fire and brimstone from the pulpit. For months, I was resistant to accepting the call to come forward for salvation at the end of the service, when the congregation would sing "Almost Persuaded." If anything, I was probably more interested in one of the pastor's teen daughters.
But after one particularly vivid sermon when Brother Frederick painted a picture of a citizen of hell reaching out an arm for help, only to have the flesh come off the bone, I took that long walk to the front of the sanctuary. "I could have fallen off my chair," said my surprised grandmother. Well, I have always liked to keep them guessing.

The baby boom generation had many firsts. We were the first to grow up with the threat of nuclear destruction, the first to grow up with a space race, and the first to grow up with television. The first program I saw on TV was Walt Disney's Davy Crockett in the mid-1950s. I watched it raptly on a neighbor's black-and-white TV, before my family had a set. Soon after, there was Howdy Doodie, Superman, Captain Midnight, and the Mickey Mouse Playhouse. We watched them all in black-and-white. TV brought old movies to the little screen that were new to us. The swashbuckling Errol Flynn in "The Adventures of Robin Hood," the late-night horror flick "The Mummy," and the fantastical "King Kong." Later we watched the comedic genius of Ernie Kovacs, and Twilight Zone, with its strange, often creepy plot twists.

In the 1950s, we listened to Elvis on the radio, and if we had a shortwave band, we would fiddle with the dial trying to listen to faint stations through the static, wondering what was out there beyond Saint Augustine. I was also an avid reader of the St. Augustine Record newspaper enjoying The Phantom, Alley Oop,

22

Li'l Abner and Dickie Dare on the comics page, as well as everything on the sports page, and the front-page news. I was interested in what was happening in St. Augustine, which was not all ancient history.

Vice President Lyndon B. Johnson paid a visit to Saint Augustine in 1963 to help kick off the 400th anniversary of the founding of the city.

When I heard that then-Vice President Lyndon Baines Johnson would be in downtown St. Augustine on March 11, 1963, I decided to go see him. Johnson was coming to town for the kickoff of plans to celebrate the 400th anniversary of the 1565 founding of the city, the nation's oldest.

When I arrived, St. George Street was already crammed with loads of townspeople, waiting to see and hear Johnson speak from the balcony of the Arrivas House. I stood far back in the crowd with my little Kodak camera. I despaired at getting a good photo as there were hundreds of people standing between me and Johnson as he gave his speech. Even so, I was able to capture several images of him from afar.

When Johnson wrapped up his comments, I prepared to go home. I didn't notice that Johnson had waded into the crowd, shaking hands. I looked up to see the 6-foot-4 Texan standing right in front of me, grinning and squinting in the late afternoon sun. His extended hand looked as large as a catcher's mitt.

"How are you doing, son?" he asked.

Stunned, I shook his hand. Later, I kicked myself for not getting a close-up photo of his craggy features. Frankly, I was afraid of making any sudden moves with the camera while those Secret Service agents were standing there, checking me out. Little could I know that I had just shaken hands with my future commander-in-chief. Nor could segregated St. Augustine know that in 1964 it would become a battleground of the Civil Rights movement, as Dr. Martin Luther King Jr. led peaceful marches downtown, near the historic slave market. The demonstrators might have been peaceful, but the whites who attacked them turned it into a long, hot summer of violence. St. Augustine came to be remembered with other epic Civil Rights battles in Mississippi, Alabama and North Carolina. The racial violence became the lead story on national TV news, and one night I went down to King Street to see for myself what was going on. I'll never forget the yelling and screams as the demonstrators marched down King Street and several white thugs swept in to attack them. Witnessing the violence, hatred and fear was an unsettling experience.

The events in St. Augustine played a role in the passage of Civil Rights legislation signed into law by Lyndon Johnson. The world was watching Saint Augustine. Dr. King later won the Noble Peace Prize for his work. The same year that LBJ visited Saint Augustine as vice president, John F. Kennedy was shot to death in Dallas. The tragedy on Nov. 22, 1963, put a pall over the country, depressed almost everyone. That weekend, there were three birthdays in the Jones household, but nobody felt like celebrating. We were watching TV when Jack Ruby stepped out of the crowd at the Dallas jail and shot Lee Harvey Oswald dead. Unbelievable.

The depressing funk continued around the country until Feb. 9, 1964, when The Beatles debuted in America, and were seen by what was at that time the largest audience in TV history. Ed Sullivan must have savored that programming stroke of genius. My whole family gathered around the TV. The Fab Four opened quietly with "All My Loving" and "Till There Was You." Then they blew the doors off with "She Loves You." With just enough snarling guitar, and a soaring chorus of "yeah, yeah, yeaahhh," it was thrilling. My little sister Sandi sort of went crazy, like girls all over the country, screaming and jumping up and down right there in the living room.

"What's wrong with Sandi?" my perplexed father kept asking.

In the second half of the show, The Beatles performed their final two songs and ratcheted up the attack with "I Saw Her Standing There," and closed with "I Want to Hold your Hand." It was exciting. More than that, it was stunning. Girls, who often seemed aloof to me, were different that night. Crazed, in a frenzy, but not aloof, at least not when it came to The Beatles. Little did we know, The Beatles had just launched a cultural revolution, and I had signed on as a fan, unable to get enough. It was as if they had some kind of cosmic channel to the hearts and minds of youth. Until then, I paid scant attention to popular music.

Even when The Beatles began turning more controversial with drug use and the claim that they were more popular than Jesus, I continued to love them for their music. John Lennon would later pose for a full-frontal nude album cover with Yoko Ono, but I still bought his music. Just because he jumped off a cliff didn't mean I would follow. Not that I didn't eventually buy a copy of "Two Virgins," and listen to the electronic noise just one time before packing it away. The Beatles were my favorites, a band of visionaries and trend setters in a universe that also came to include the Rolling Stones, The Who, Bob Dylan, Simon and Garfunkle, the Loving Spoonful, and so many others.

My high school years were also a golden time for hitting the library. I soaked up biographies, classics like "Moby Dick" and histories like the Civil War epic "Andersonville" by Pulitzer Prize winner MacKinlay Kantor. I didn't realize until many years later, that Kantor had also written a book titled "Glory For Me," about returning World War II vets. The book provided the inspiration for one of my favorite movies "The Best Years of Our Lives," released in 1946.

When I graduated from St. Augustine High School in 1965, it was with an all-white class, a class that stood as one when the band played "Dixie" during pep rallies. The thought did enter my mind that maybe we were missing something by not having integrated schools. Occasionally, a student would transfer into Saint Augustine High School from the North where schools were integrated. What's it like? I asked. "It's no big deal. We're all just students," they would say. A few years later, integration would finally come to Saint Augustine High School.

My family was just relieved that I finished high school in four years. I skipped college after getting my high school diploma in 1965. What else could I do? My family had no money, and nobody was offering scholarships to academic laggards like me.

6 - Freedom

For high school graduation in 1965, my father gave me a 1956 hardtop Buick. It was canary yellow with a straight-stick transmission, a clutch, and eight cylinders under the hood. I couldn't have been happier or prouder, even if it was a nine-year-old car. It was big and heavy and held its own in traffic.

My first summer job after graduating from high school was spent working as an aid with a survey crew in Hastings.

"Buick" was another way to spell "freedom." Now, I could explore, go fishing, and drive to work.

My first job was as a summer aide on a survey crew mapping farm fields for the Soil Conservation Service. It was a three-month job — perhaps part of LBJ's "Great Society" program. It was intended to put a little money in the pockets of youth from low-income families. I was the stick guy, basically a flunky who held the survey stick, and jumped on and off the running board of a pickup truck as it cross-crossed huge farm fields. My job was to place the survey stick next to wooden stakes in a grid that covered the field. Surveyor Arlo Carter would look through his transit, and wave, signaling when he had recorded the reading. We would then move on to the next stake.

It was a hot, dirty work.

A lost world: the family farm in Spuds, Fla., shown in 1927. The family went bust during the Great Depression. The painting is by my great-aunt Louise Parks. The horses are named Midnight and Lightning. The cow was named Bonnie. My great-grandmother's little dog, Ponzie, is shown at bottom left.

It was fun.

And, it was exhilarating; after all, I had been a chicken wrangler and hard-luck gardener at home, and a reluctant student in high school. Now, I was able to escape my crowded home life with all its drama.

Arlo was a folksy man with a chaw of tobacco, a little straw hat, and a sense of humor. He was a good man, who a had a University of Florida degree, but you wouldn't know it. Arlo was also the best first boss I could have had. He took a fatherly interest in me, encouraging me to go to college and earn a degree. He also jokingly warned me to stay away from his daughters. I promised to do both, but I knew that I was prime draft material, and college might have to wait.

28

Arlo's sidekick, Sammy Lane, was a country boy a couple of years older than me, who looked every inch the handsome cowboy. He later became a St. Johns County deputy sheriff and married the girl who lived next door to me. The banter inside the U.S. government pickup truck as we drove from one survey job to the next was funny, off-color, and uplifting. Surprising, too, considering that I had little idea until then that grownups talked a lot like high school boys. I learned it was possible to work hard and have fun at the same time. Dressed in a short-sleeve shirt, cowboy hat and blue jeans, I was in my element.

Arlo turned the data we collected into maps that farmers could use to sculpt their fields. When the growers opened their artesian wells, water would flow to all the rows of potato and cabbage without use of electrical pumps. I was aware that I was tromping through the same fields in Spuds, Elkton, and Hastings, where my grandparents and great-grandparents had farmed, and suffered financial ruin during the Great Depression. When the surveying job ended after a few months, I bagged groceries, before getting a tip about a job at the Florida Times-Union newspaper in Jacksonville.

My neighbor, a printer, knew that I wanted to be an artist and told me the newspaper had an opening. By the time I interviewed, the artist job had been filled. But they had an opening for an apprentice pressman and I took it. I liked my time at the Times-Union, and my interaction with the columnists and reporters. They were characters unlike anyone else I had met. At that time, type was set manually by a crew of linotype operators, who swore better than they typed. It was my job to place the hot type in galleys, being careful not to drop any of it or get it out of order, and to run proofs which we sent upstairs via a vacuum tube to the newsroom for the editors to read. I learned to read the lead type upside down and backwards and would have learned a lot more about the operation. Except that the newspaper experience would be short-lived.

But while it lasted, I was able to drive between Jacksonville and Saint Augustine in my old Buick, and to go everywhere else until one day I tore the clutch up racing another driver on U.S. 1. My father was not happy with me. We replaced the clutch, quickly getting me back on the road. His disapproval meant I would not dare tear up another clutch. I was able to visit my mother more often, but I was oblivious to the challenges she was facing. All I knew was that she appeared to me to be living the American dream: a real nice suburban house with a swimming pool, a convertible in the driveway, and a big boat in the yard. Appearances can be deceiving. After leaving my father, she would marry three more times. Her second

My mother, shown here on a deep-sea fishing trip in 1966, appeared to be living the American dream. But she faced a horror I knew nothing about. (Jones family collection)

and third marriages ended badly. Those husbands were hitters, who turned mean when they drank. I did not know. For a short time, my sister Phyllis lived with her. Years later, she told me that there was a lot of fighting in the house. One time, Phyllis hid Thelma in a closet, fearing that a drunk blind man would try to kill her.

On another occasion, Thelma called her baby sister, Verona, and asked if she knew how to stop a bad nosebleed. Even with the hell that home life had become, Thelma put up a good front. Too many women have had to put up good fronts over the years. Tragically, the dimensions of the problem came into even sharper focus in 2017 and 2018 with women coming forward to report abuse at the hands of rich and powerful men nationwide.

During her years in Jacksonville, my mother worked as a waitress in the restaurant at Imeson Airport, and her husband worked as a general aviation mechanic. Through their connections, I got to take my first flight, in a little single-engine propeller aircraft, that flew from Jacksonville to Waycross, Ga., and back. It was a revelation seeing the earth from the sky for the first time and experiencing the sensation of the

30

aircraft climbing into the air. Even better, in December 1965, my mother heard that the Dave Clark Five, one of the great British Invasion bands, would be passing through Imeson Airport.

Thelma arranged for Phyllis, Sandi, and I to meet the band as they walked across the tarmac to board their airplane. My sisters got autographs and I got to photograph the band. In their mod haircuts, and neatly tailored suits, I thought these were some of the coolest looking, most sophisticated dudes I had ever seen, even though lead singer Mike Smith had a few pimples like me.

My sister Sandi spent her junior high school and high school years with Thelma and has a more fully formed view of her during those years.

Mike Smith, lead singer of the Dave Clark Five, signs an autograph for my sister, Sandi, (in the plaid dress) at Jacksonville's Imeson Airport in 1965.
Photo by the author

"One of the things I loved about our mother was she was a bit of a free spirit. From the convertibles she owned and enjoyed to letting me be a teenager. She didn't overreact when mistakes were made but did acknowledge them," Sandi said.

"As a hard-working waitress in the only restaurant at the Imeson airport in Jacksonville before the days a new airport was built, she came in contact with people from all walks of life. This setting provided perhaps the moment I was most proud of her. "It was a shameful time in our country in the early 1960s when segregation was rampant and ugly. One day The Rev. Martin Luther King Jr. came into the restaurant and sat down for a meal. None of the other waitresses wanted to serve him. Our mother thought nothing of it and went right over to take care of him. She saw him as a customer. It's sad to think that should be a proud moment that she served a black man but in those days it was a big deal. I'm proud she had the honor to serve such a man and proud of her as my mother," Sandi said.

Even though I might not have lived with my mother for half my childhood, we managed to stay in touch, and I knew that she loved me.

Never would that mean more than in 1966, when I had a date history.

7 – Olive drab

Light weapons infantry training, Fort Ord, 1966. I am in the third row, fourth from right.

The United States is a nation of irreverent, nonconformist, free-thinking, authority-hating, freedom-loving people.Given our choice, we would make love, not to war. Not that we always have a choice. I came home from work at the Florida Times-Union one evening and my stepmother, Margie, was standing in the living room, waiting to hand me a letter. She watched intently as I opened the envelope. It was from the Selective Service System. Never before had Margie waited to hand me my mail. This letter would be life changing.

It started with the one word that a whole generation of young men feared: "Greeting." Mincing no words, the letter from my local draft board continued:

"You are hereby ordered for induction into the Armed Forces of the United States, and to report at Greyhound Bus Station, 162 San Marco Avenue, St. Augustine, Florida on Feb. 9, 1966 at 7:50 a.m. for forwarding to an Armed Forces Induction Station."

The letter was dated Jan. 17, 1966, meaning that I had about three weeks before I would be entering the service.

The Gulf of Tonkin Resolution, signaling the escalation of hostilities in Vietnam, was more than a year old, and it was clear that the fighting would not be halted anytime soon.

Basic training, Fort Benning, Ga.: This photo was an insider joke between my father and me. I had seen a photo of him during his World War II Army days posed on a ladder just like this one.

American leaders were fearful that if Vietnam fell to the communists, it would be the first of many dominoes to fall in Asia, perhaps tipping the balance of power forever against the Free World. They were willing to spend American capital and use the draft to fight the Viet Cong.

When I went to show my draft notice to the shop foreman, he just somberly shook his head. He knew what the paper was in my hand before I could unfold it.

"I have seen too many of those," he said quietly.

I felt powerless with my freedom about to be ripped away. Yes, opening a letter from the local draft board felt like a moment of impending doom. I set out to do an end-run around the draft, like so many others had done by enrolling in college or joining the Army Reserve or National Guard. But it was too late. All the nearby Reserve and Guard units were full and had a waiting list. I was headed to the armed services, even though I wasn't sure which one. Inevitably, with all those reminders of honorable military service in my family, I wondered whether I would measure up.

In the family albums, there were black-and-white snapshots fading to sepia of my father in uniform in some of the places he had been. Many times, I asked him about his time in the Army. Unlike some fathers who never talked about their experiences, he would answer my questions, and how his mechanic skills served him well during his time in the service. I, on the other hand, had no particular skill. I seemed destined for the infantry. I was just a warm, healthy body, and apparently that was enough.

I was drafted into the U.S. Army in February 1966 as the fighting in the Vietnam War grew more ferocious by the month. My best friend went to Canada to avoid the draft. It would be many years before I would see him again. Although I didn't share my thoughts with my family, I knew there was a chance I would not survive my time in the Army. And even if I did, my two-year obligation as a draftee seemed like an eternity.

"You don't have to keep my car for me," I told my father. "You can use it or sell it."

My father drove me to the St. Augustine Greyhound bus station on Feb. 9, 1966, where I joined other inductees bound for basic training at Fort Benning, Ga. We processed into the Army at the induction station in Jacksonville, where the medics yelled at and harassed the inductees. Taking the vision test, a medic told me, "Man, you're blind as a bat." So what if my vision wasn't 20-20? At 20-40, I was hardly blind. Nobody said anything about my flat feet, even though I pointed them out to the

35

medics. The St. Augustine draftees who completed their processing that day were drafted into the Marines, including my high school classmate Ricky Osteen who would die in Vietnam before the year was out.

Overnight, the U.S. government put us up in a seedy hotel in Jacksonville. A bellhop came to the door and asked if we wanted to "buy a piece of trim." I had never heard the term, but I knew what he was talking about. "No thank you," we all said, suspecting a scam. I completed my processing the next day and passed my physical examination. I raised my right hand to take the oath to defend the Constitution and stepped forward into the United States Army.

When the bus pulled up to the front gate at Fort Benning, Ga., on Feb. 10, 1966, carrying me and the other newbies from Saint Augustine, it was nighttime. Rain fell in sheets. A sentry, wearing a steel pot, a poncho gleaming in the rain, and carrying an M-14 rifle slung upside down over one shoulder, patrolled the Home of the Infantry in the gloom. A smirking Army buck sergeant climbed up the steps of the bus and greeted us at the gate: "Well kiss my dick," he said. Yes, we were in the Army, and in the wrong place if we expected a friendly reception.

Everyone yelled at us: the cooks who slopped food onto our trays in the mess hall, and the supply sergeants who issued fatigues, ill-fitting dress greens complete with a poplin shirt, dull, black low-quarter shoes and Army boots. We would be expected to quickly learn how to spit shine the footwear to a mirror finish. The drill sergeants, who would be our constant companions for the next two months, yelled at us, too.

Even before we were issued our uniforms, a fight broke out in the entrance of the barracks. Two of the biggest guys in the company, one black and one white, exchanged insults and punches, grabbed each other, and fell to the floor, before being pulled apart. In 1966, integration was still new to many in the South, even though the military had been integrated since the early 1950s.

Aside from that one incident, the trainees quickly learned to get-along. Our lives had been turned upside down, and we had a lot of adjusting to do. We were being told when to get up, how to make our bunks, how to shine our boots, how to wear the new olive drab uniform, how to stand in formation, and how to march with an M-14.

"The other boys from Saint Augustine who were on the bus with me, were put in other platoons. I don't know anyone here, but I've started making friends. They have us cleaning barracks, policing the grounds, and marching. I was ready to quit and come home after the first day, but since they cut all my hair off, I've changed my mind," I wrote my family, tongue-in-cheek.

We learned how to march in formation with an M-14, how to do close order drill, and that when given the command, "right face," not to "face left." A mistake like that would lead to an insult from the drill sergeant, "your military right, troop," and maybe pushups. Soon enough we would all get our share of KP -- kitchen police -- which meant peeling an endless mountain of potatoes or washing pots and pans. We also walked fire guard at night, making sure the furnace was fed with coal and that the barracks didn't catch fire. Then there were the long marches in full field gear. Even so, basic training seemed to agree with me. While many of the trainees lost weight, I liked Army chow and gained 18 pounds.

I wanted to do well. At the induction station, I had gone from not wanting to be in the Army to not wanting to flunk my physical exam. In basic training, I wanted not to just get by, but to excel. And I did. The first time we took the physical combat proficiency test (PCPT) — the one-mile run, 25-meter low crawl, the run, dodge and jump, the parallel bars and the hand grenade throw — I scored 365 out of 500 points. Passing, but not a very good score, which reflected my uncertainty about what we were supposed to be doing.

When we took the test a second time, this time for record, I knew exactly what to do, and attacked the course. One of the scorers came over to me with one event left — the mile run — and told me that I was high scorer in the company. All I needed to do to win the PCPT trophy was to max the mile run. I jumped out front and led the company to the finish line, guaranteeing that I would win the PCPT trophy with 483 points out of a possible 500. Afterward, the company commander came to the barracks to shake my hand and congratulate me. It dawned on me that while I might not be some kind of super athlete, I was fit enough to hold my own in the Army.

I also qualified as a sharpshooter with the M-14 on the rifle range. That wasn't the top badge. Expert was. But it wasn't marksman, either, the lowest qualifying badge, Or worse yet, a bolo, one who failed to qualify on the rifle range. Prior to being drafted, I had never fired a rifle. I was happy to be a sharpshooter.

One night the company commander called a small group of us into the orderly room and told us our GT (intelligence) scores were high enough that we should consider taking the Officer Candidate Test. "Anyone who isn't interested in taking the OCT, get out of my office," said the company commander, a tall, stern young second lieutenant with perfect military bearing. He looked every inch the warrior in his crisply starched, tailored fatigues. Half the group was not impressed. Or maybe they just didn't want to be in the Army a day longer than necessary. They saluted and left the orderly room.

I stayed.

"If you are fortunate enough to complete the six months of Officer Candidate School, you will be commissioned as second lieutenants, and incur a two-year service commitment from the date of commissioning," our company commander said, his tone softening. Well, why not? Let's take the OCT. I have nothing to lose, I thought. So, I took the OCT, scored well, and reported to an Army board of officers for an interview in my dress greens, spit-shined low quarter shoes and gleaming brass.

I answered a few questions and was dismissed. My only slip up was at the end of the interview, when I did an about face, as I prepared to leave. I caught myself and realized that I had not saluted. I stopped, executed a crisp about face, looked squarely at the board, and rendered my best hand salute. I passed the board.

Had I not elected to go to OCS, the Army would have sent me to air traffic controller school. Surprising, because as a draftee, I figured I would be headed straight to the infantry.

But after I was selected for OCS, my sergeants informed me that I would not be going to air traffic control school after all, but rather to light weapons infantry training at Fort Ord, Calif., for the "leadership skills" that I would learn -- a benefit to anyone aspiring to be an officer. There was also an implied promise: wash out of OCS and you're going to Vietnam as an infantryman.

At Fort Ord, I continued to excel in my new military career, getting a perfect score on the final infantry proficiency test. I was awarded a Zippo cigarette lighter with a Sixth Army patch, inscribed with my perfect score, one of about 20 in the company. Never mind that I did not smoke.

Our company at Fort Ord was an elite unit. All of my classmates were heading to either airborne training or to OCS. When I look back on a photo of that group of infantry trainees, I wonder how many went to Vietnam, and how many returned alive. I had filled out a dream sheet at Fort Ord, listing my OCS preferences. Number-one was signal, followed by infantry, and then armor. When the company clerk posted the assignments on the unit bulletin board, I learned I would be heading to Signal OCS at Fort Gordon, Ga.

8 - OCS

FORT GORDON, Ga.

Officers candidate faces show the strain as they go for a run in early 1967 at Fort Gordon, Ga. Because I was one of the best runners in the platoon, I served as a road guard blocking traffic and would then run to catch up with the rest of my platoon.

"**G**et in the front-leaning rest position. Give me 25 pushups," the tactical officer, Lt. Chuck Wetmore, ordered. I dove to the ground, along with the other officer candidates in my platoon. The grass drilling had begun." Get on your back," Wetmore would say. Then in rapid-fire, dispassionate, almost robotic order: "On your belly, on your side, on your head, on your back." Candidates struggled to keep up with Wetmore's relentless grass drilling. He might grass drill us because we screwed up, or for no reason at all.

It was all part of the horror that was Signal Officer Candidate School, intended to weed out the weakest among us. The strategy worked. Several candidates quit the first day. Candidates were forbidden to walk, so we ran everywhere. Whenever we ran in formation, we sang innocuous marching songs like "Bo Diddley" or "She Wore a Yellow Ribbon." But never, "Where Have All the Flowers Gone," a depressing hit song about the futility of war.

Our training didn't end at sundown.

We ran in full combat dress at night – fatigues, combat boots, helmet, field pack and M-14 rifle -- from the OCS barracks to post headquarters and back again, a distance of about three miles. If we displeased Wetmore, he would make us repeat the run, or worse yet, low crawl until our elbows bled from scraping against the hard Georgia clay. We came to view Wetmore with a mixture of fear, hatred, fascination, and respect. Among ourselves, we referred to him as "Ivan the Terrible." By turns, his pale blue eyes seemed cold, or cruel. He reveled in his power as tac. He ordered push-ups at every opportunity. An "opportunity" might include smiling at the wrong time, or for no reason at all, such as owning a car, or "being ugly."

In the mess hall, we ate "square meals" while sitting on the front four inches of our chairs. The fork traveled in a 90-degree angle from the plate to the candidate's mouth. We could not talk or look around. Any head movement, especially toward the plate, caught the Wetmore's attention. "Dive bombing" the food was punishable by 100 pushups outside the mess hall in the gravel. We had five minutes to eat. Any offender caught dive bombing would have to forfeit the rest of his meal while he did pushups. Many washed out of the program because of stress, harassment, or failure to meet academic and physical standards.

We heard that Signal OCS had the highest washout rate of any OCS because of the physical demands combined with electrical engineer-grade academics. We were up daily before sunrise, cleaning the barracks, and waxing the floor until it gleamed. We polished every toilet, faucet and piece of tile in the latrine. Every cigarette butt can was filled with two inches of water, and carefully hung on posts along the center aisle of the barracks. We checked the alignment of spit-shined boots under our bunk beds with string pulled tight between the bunk legs.

We could never give too much attention to the barracks or our personal appearance. We disassembled our belt buckles and shined them inside and out with Brasso. We changed uniforms several times a day to keep the starch fresh and the creases sharp. We constantly dusted our lacquered helmet liners and boots to keep them gleaming. Inevitably, our efforts fell short, and the tacs would "nuke" the barracks, turning over bunks, emptying laundry bags, stepping on boots. We would have to put everything back in order by the time lights went back on the next morning.

Wearing the orange ascot, helmet stripes, and leadership tabs as a Signal OCS senior candidate: less than three weeks to graduation as a second lieutenant.

We were confined to the OCS area for six months, and not allowed to go to movies, snack bars, or anywhere else for that matter. There were two exceptions. When he advanced from being basic candidates to junior candidates, we were allowed a party to celebrate in Augusta. Better yet, each candidate drew a blind date from the Medical College of Georgia. My date was a lovely blue-eyed nursing student with long brown hair named Lynn Davis. We hit it off right away, and exchanged addresses, promising to write. The second exception was for the Christmas holiday, when we were allowed to take leave and go home for a week. We paid dearly when we returned.

The tacs immediately had us running in full combat gear. A candidate or two collapsed. But there was no lasting harm done. It seemed as if our tacs were angered that we had been given leave. We quickly settled back into the relentless pursuit of the gold bar.

In the evenings, we polished our boots, and studied, even after lights out with a blanket pulled over our heads, using a flashlight. We spent our days in the classroom, where exhausted candidates struggled to stay awake. Anyone caught nodding off would be sent outside to do pushups or be grass drilled.

We took a water break after going on our first run after Christmas break. My friend Bob, at right, was one of the best candidates in the company.

I continued to advance with my OCS class to senior candidate status. With the gold bar of a second lieutenant within grasp – just three weeks from graduation – I flunked a critical test. Wetmore called me into his office and said that I could either take a two-month setback or I could wash out.

Humiliated, I responded: " Wash me out. I'll go to Vietnam."

But Wetmore surprised me.

"Jim, you should take the setback. You can do two months on your head. It's nothing. You'll make it," Wetmore said. He wasn't gloating and there was no sarcasm. I was stunned. Wetmore had put aside his Ivan the Terrible mask to offer a moment of encouragement to someone he thought had potential. I swallowed my pride and took the setback. I would study. I would not fail again. From my mother, I received an encouraging telegraph. In

my letters home, I would often include an OCS phrase: "drive on." In the telegraph, my mother told me she loved me, and urged me to "drive on." I did. The second time around, I passed all the tests.

In April 1967, at age 20, I received my commission as a second lieutenant. I was happy, proud, and in disbelief that I had succeeded. It was one of the best days of my life. I had come a long way from January 1966, when I was an ink-stained press apprentice, punching a clock in Jacksonville. My proud family drove up from Florida to Fort Gordon to watch my class get our gold bars.

Brand-new second lieutenant

My commission was a special source of pride for my dad. During World War II, he scored well enough to go to OCS, but decided against it because he had only a sixth-grade education. All of his entreaties for me to stay in high school made sense, not that I needed persuading. I had never given any thought to dropping out of school. My mother, who had encouraged me after my setback with a telegram that said "Drive-on, I still love you," was there, too, to pin on my gold bars. After graduation, I had 30 days of leave.

Lynn Davis, who had met at an OCS party, went on to a mission job in Africa. I was headed to a signal battalion in Germany. Lynn and I exchanged letters a few times. Like two ships in the night, we went on to different worlds, never to meet again. But I never forgot her. Or a special moment of beauty, grace, and civility at that OCS party in Augusta.

9 - Germany

It's a small world.

Field training exercise, Germany, 1968.

My route to Germany took me on a commercial airline flight from Jacksonville, Fla., to New York. I stayed in the transient officers' quarters at Fort Dix, N. J., for a day or two, while awaiting my flight to Frankfurt. The front desk assigned a private to carry my bags to my room upstairs. The private turned out to a high school classmate from Saint Augustine, Fla. It was a big surprise for both of us. Ironically, his father was my father's boss. Now, he was carrying my bags. Think about that.

"How are you doing Frankie?" I asked.

He smiled, seemingly bewildered that he had run into a high school classmate who was now a second lieutenant. I wished him well, and said it was nice to meet a friend so far from home. Gee, I thought to myself, the Army really is the greatest equal opportunity employer.

I was at Fort Dix long enough to take a bus to Manhattan. I had never been to New York City, so I put on my civilian clothes and went downtown to do a little exploring. For a guy who once helped survey cabbage fields in Hastings, Fla., seeing the skyscapers in Manhattan for the first time was a dazzling and dizzying experience. I was peering into a Manhattan deli window, watching a pizza maker toss a spinning wheel of dough into the air, when a neatly dressed man in a coat and tie approached me and offered to show me around town. He said he was a local university professor and asked what I did.

"I'm an Army lieutenant heading to Germany. I'm in New York for the first time," I said.

He seemed like a nice, well-mannered guy. I welcomed the opportunity to have a local show me the sights. I was so naive. After we had gone a few blocks, he made a pass at me.

"No thank you. I think you have me confused with someone else," I said.

He apologized as I walked away. So, that's my first memory of New York: dizzyingly tall buildings, deli pizza, and a gay man making a pass at me.

***

The flight to Frankfurt was long but less eventful. From Frankfurt I took the train to Stuttgart, where a driver in an Army three-quarter ton truck picked me up at the hauptbahnhof — the main train station — and drove me and my duffle bag to Ludwigsburg.

My first assignment was as the assistant platoon leader of the cable and wire platoon of Company B, 34th Signal Battalion in Ludwigsburg, just north of Stuttgart. Several of my OCS classmates were already assigned to the 34th Signal Battalion, including Earl Tingle who had become the S-2 officer. Jack Jones, Vince Jones, and Bill Lublin were also there, assigned to one platoon or another. There was a degree of comfort in that, and I quickly began to learn the local terrain. I could walk the mile or two from my BOQ (bachelor officers 'quarters) at Flak Kasern to

Krabbenloch Kasern, where Company B headquarters was located.

I enjoyed greeting the local Germans I passed with "guten morgan" (good morning) as I walked along the little road between the two Army compounds. Eager, hungry, and green. That pretty well described me. I wanted to do well and show what an OCS grad could do. So far, I had gotten everything I had listed on my "dream sheet." The officer candidate school of my choice and assignment to Germany. I was a second lieutenant, something I could not have aspired to two years earlier when I was just out of high school and working in the composing room of the Florida Times Union in Jacksonville. With a two-year commitment from this point on, I had probably dodged having to go to Vietnam. My goal was to complete my Army service and get to work on my college degree.

I was enjoying the postcard scenery of Germany. There was nothing back home in flat woods Florida like the Alps, the castles, and the cobblestone streets. The country was tidy, green, and modern, even though some buildings still carried the scars of World War II. Being a red-blooded young man, I couldn't help but notice that Germany seemed to have plenty of beautiful women, too. It was more than anyone drafted into the Army in 1966 had a right to expect.

Yet, I had a feeling that something was not right in Ludwigsburg. There was talk about a recent court martial of an enlisted man who who had stabbed another GI to death in the barracks.

"Had I seen the autopsy pictures?" someone asked.

No. and I don't care to, I replied. Two lieutenants in our battalion were court martialed, one for claiming an allowance he wasn't entitled to, and the other for trying to get out of the Army without completing his military obligation.

During the next 13 months, I could not seem to advance beyond being an assistant platoon leader for another second lieutenant, who might outrank me by just a week or two. Mostly, we seemed to spend our time in the field, running communications cable through the forests to connect communications sites, or establishing radio links. Adding an element of realism to these

48

field training exercises was the fact that our bitter communist enemies, Soviet and East German forces, were out there, just east of the "Iron Curtain." Furthermore, we were placed on alert during the Six Day War when Israel fought off Arab forces on three sides, and occupied the Golan Heights, the West Bank and Sinai. The question was whether that conflict would spread and become much larger? Fortunately, it did not. During our field training exercises, we did not rest until we had established our communications, even if that meant working around the clock without sleep for two or three days. There is no greater pressure on a Signal Corps officer than for a general somewhere to be yelling about his communications not working.

It was during one such exhausting field training exercise that I had an unnerving experience. Walking across a darkened field one night in the German woods, I saw Nazi soldiers approaching in the gloom. This seemed very real to me and my heart was pounding. Finally someone shined a flashlight on me and called my name. It was another lieutenant from my battalion, and it was 1967 again — not 1945. Had I seen ghosts from World War II? Or was I hallucinating from sleep deprivation? I never mentioned my experience to another soul for good reason. I didn't want anyone thinking I was crazy.

In all, I would be assigned to three different platoons during my 13 months in Germany. The final assignment — to the combat support platoon in Schwabisch Hall — was the best.

I sketched this German tower during a field training exercise in April 1967. Down on the ground is a U.S. Army 2 1/2-ton truck with a communications van mounted on the back. At the top of the tower is an antenna. To me the sketch says "Signal" and "creativity" in taking advantage of local terrain features.

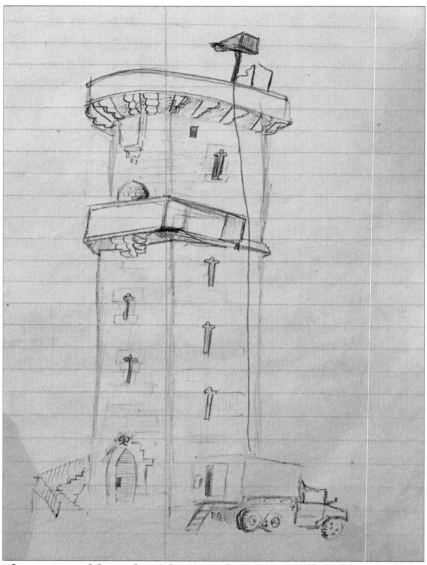

There I would work with OCS classmate Bill Lublin. But before I joined Bill, I requested assignment to Vietnam. I felt I needed a change, and I wanted to stop practicing for war when the United

States was actually fighting one. Bill was a natural leader. He had my best interests at heart and encouraged me with constructive criticism and a strong efficiency report. When Bill's mother, Mary, and sister, Marti, visited from Norfolk, Va., we became friends, too.

I bought a 10-year-old Mercedes Benz sedan from another G.I. for $100 and drove up the autobahn to Cologne, where I saw the famous Dom Cathedral. I enjoyed going to the local eateries and having schnitzel with a German beer. There was some good news when I was called to battalion headquarters and promoted to first lieutenant. Things were going so well that I had almost forgotten that I had requested assignment to Vietnam.

Then, I received my orders to report to Vietnam just as the Viet Cong's Tet Offensive erupted in early 1968. Suddenly, it looked like all the rosy forecasts about the war being won were wrong. Making the bad news even more personal was the death of Leon Huber, a classmate at Saint Augustine High School, after serving nearly a full year in Vietnam. Leon was a generator operator caught out in the open at Khe Sanh by enemy fire. He was a member of the 1st Signal Brigade, the unit to which I had been assigned in Vietnam. Leon and I had been in the same 10th grade English class, and I remember him coming to class with his "Meet the Beatles" album, wearing Beatle boots, and sporting a mop-top haircut. It didn't seem possible that such a funny, friendly free-spirit was gone.

All I could hope for as I prepared to head for Vietnam was that I had learned enough that I would be a good officer in the combat zone. I didn't want to make any stupid mistakes and I didn't want to get anyone killed. I worried about the thing that every soldier worries about. Would I have enough guts to do my job when everything turned to shit? As I processed out of Germany, a sergeant gave me a bit of advice.

"Lieutenant, keep your head down" he said.

10 - Vietnam

My family was all smiles.

It was just a brave front. I was home on a 30-day leave after leaving Germany. They knew I was heading for Vietnam. Margie, my stepmother, fixed me up with a date with a local girl. We got along so well that we were together the rest of my leave. My mother fixed all my favorite meals, including her Saint Augustine-style fried shrimp with cornmeal breading. My grandmother made my favorite dessert, banana pudding.

I took a photo of the Haight Ashbury sign, but not the hippies, in 1968.

Mama cried when I flew to the West Coast, sure that something terrible would happen to me. When I got to California, before reporting to Travis Air Force Base for my flight, I took a side trip to San Francisco. I visited the Haight Ashbury section to see real, live flower children. I also made a stop at one of the city's famous topless bars. Neither experience lived up to my expectations. I came away underwhelmed.

Our flight to Vietnam was aboard a chartered Flying Tiger airliner filled with enlisted men. As a first lieutenant, I was the ranking officer on the plane. We flew north from Travis Air Force Base to Anchorage, Alaska. Our flight took the polar route over Alaska's glaciers to Japan, and finally to Bien Hoa Air Force Base, Vietnam. The plane touched down at Bien Hoa in the middle of the night. We were aware that this was the Land of the Dragon, in the Year of the Monkey, 1968. We sat in hushed silence in our wrinkled khakis, the moist heat of Vietnam filling the cabin, until an Air Force sergeant boarded the plane and told us what to do in the event of an enemy attack. As we hustled off the plane, we saw an infantry platoon, tired, and dirty, sprawled on the ground. They had just returned from a patrol. They watched us, the replacements, getting off the plane the same disdainful way a varsity football team might look at the JV.

We boarded buses and peered through mesh-screened windows as we drove through the darkened streets of Bien Hoa. Military police in Jeeps provided the escort. It was after curfew. We didn't see a soul. Arriving at the replacement battalion, supply sergeants issued us blankets and sheets. We flopped exhausted onto our bunks. It had been a brutal 24 hours in the air.

The next morning, we saw Vietnam in the daylight for the first time: rows of unpainted wooden barracks sitting on rolling hills. Grass and trees had been bulldozed

Handbook issued to American troops in Vietnam to explain local customs and culture.

away, exposing the rocky, red soil underneath.

Someone had erected a post with signs pointing to Atlanta, New York, Los Angeles and other places back home, thousands of miles away. We sweated it out for a day or two in the replacement battalion, waiting for assignment to the field.

The wait was excruciating.

We heard the sound of helicopter rotors beating through the sky. It was a sound we would hear daily as long as we were in Vietnam. In the coming months, we would experience other sensations and sounds that remain with us: the crash of incoming mortar fire at night, M-60 and .50 caliber machine gun fire; the quake of B-52 carpet bombing, dust rising off in the distance. In August, 1968, I was assigned to Can Tho as assistant operations officer – the assistant S-3 – in the headquarters of the 52nd Signal Battalion.

Waterfront in Sadec, one of the 52nd Signal Battalion's
Signal sites, and one of the first locations that I visited in

From Can Tho, the battalion-controlled companies in Can Tho, Dong Tam, Long Xuyen, Vinh Long, and Soc Trang, providing communications to all of IV Corps, the southernmost military region in Vietnam. The 9th Infantry Division provided the tip of the spear in IV Corps.

Can Tho was a teeming city, the largest in Vietnam's Mekong Delta. Its rough, muddy streets were filled with soldiers, refugees, trucks, bicycles, and even the occasional water buffalo. The battalion was headquartered in the former Bank of Indochina building, with fortress-like masonry walls and echoing spaces,

54

near the Bassac River. The old bank building had dark wooden counters and slowly turning fans suspended from the tall ceilings. Outside, armed guards stood watch behind sandbagged strong points and barbed wire.

Can Tho had a thriving black market in the notorious Ben Xe Moi red light district, which was off-limits to G.I.'s. Vietnamese merchants openly sold pilfered U.S. jungle boots and C rations on the black market. Rumor had it that the VC were collecting

protection money from the local businesses, accounting for the lack of attacks on the city in the few months since Tet of 1968. Was the money being used to finance attacks elsewhere? Perhaps. Or maybe it was quiet because the VC units had been so decimated during Tet they couldn't mount any kind of a large attack.

In my first week or so, I accompanied the battalion commander to several signal sites north of Can Tho, including Sadec and Vinh Long. Company C, our unit in Vinh Long, had just sustained an attack and casualties. A mortar round hit a barracks full of sleeping men. The sight of the blood covering the floor was sickening.

In jungle fatigues in Vietnam.

I was assistant to the operations office, Major Leland Jost, a straight-talking, hard-working signal officer who knew his stuff. His gruff demeanor was balanced by a hearty sense of humor. I recognized that he was just the medicine that a greenhorn first lieutenant like me needed. The days were long for Jost and me, 6:30 a.m. – 11 p.m. seven days a week, and sometimes even longer. But no one complained because we knew that the guys humping through the jungles and rice paddies were putting their lives on the line every day. The battalion offered everything in the way of communications to support the 9th Infantry Division, as well as Special Forces, attack helicopter units, engineers, and Military Assistance Command advisors in the region. Battalion signalmen operated dial telephone exchanges, communications centers where secure teletype messages were sent and received, multi-channel radio links, high frequency radio teletype, and more.

One of the most unusual operations was providing communications support to the Mobile Riverine Force, which sailed up and down the brown-water rivers in the region with soldiers onboard ready to respond to hot spots. It was a challenge learning to rotate the antennas to follow the USS Benewah as it cruised the waters of Vietnam. The multi-channel radios that supplied communications to the Benewah were point-to-point. If the antennas weren't correctly rotated to track the ship, the communications link would be broken.

Jost and I spent relatively little time in the bank building. Mostly we were in the field troubleshooting problems

"The day generally consists of a series of crisises with radio links going off the air through operator neglect, faulty equipment or enemy activity," I wrote my mother in September of 1968.

Operator neglect was more the exception than the rule, as our signalmen were skilled and creative in making the communications system work. Aside from the work, the GIs found ways to pass the time, including keeping short-timers calendars, counting the days until R 'n 'R when we would get to let off steam in places like Taipei, Bangkok, or Tokyo. We would also pencil in the date when we would complete our 12-month tour of duty in Vietnam. Officially, it was DEROS, Date Eligible for Return from Overseas. Unofficially, there was another acronym, FIGMO, "fuck it, got my orders." That December I would be spending my second Christmas away from home. A year ago, I had spent my Christmas in Stuttgart. Now I was in the Mekong Delta.

Chaplain Joel Embry had a Christmas surprise for us.

Unknown to us, Embry sent letters to each of our families asking for a photo to "give us a lift" during the holiday.

"We know that we cannot be with our wives and families personally, but we can be together in spirit for Christmas," he wrote.

During a party at Christmas he showed us color slides of our families. We chuckled at the image of one of the dads, looking like a Hatfield or McCoy with a shotgun in his lap. The officers whistled at the images of my pretty, blond sisters. There were warm, full hearts in that room in Can Tho for Christmas of 1968, and maybe a few misty eyes as well. About that same time, some of the senior officers began encouraging me to make the Army a career, and to take command of a company. It was heady stuff for someone like me, who was hungry for encouragement and direction. I hesitated on accepting a command, wondering whether I was ready. But my bosses finally said, look, in January you're going to take over Company D in Soc Trang. That's the way that it is!

11 – The Delta

In December 1968, the battalion commander told me to get ready to assume command of Company D, the southern-most U.S. Signal company in Vietnam. Soon afterward, I joined him and the outgoing Company D commander on a helicopter tour of signal sites. The tour was designed to acquaint me with Company D sites, as well as a few others that were in other companies. We visited Chau Doc and Chi Lang along the Cambodian border as well as to

Company D had a four-man radio relay site at Gia Rai between Bac Lieu and Ca Mau. The day that the battalion commander visited there were five in his party. Shown above are Lt. Col. Gerald R. Jennings, Capt. John McDougle, Sergeant Major Kimbrough, and 1st Sgt. Roy Yonemura. I took the photo in front of a Vietnamese church as local children gathered around at Christmas time.

sites in the far south, including the fishing village of Rach Gia on Vietnam's west coast, and Gia Rai, a tiny radio relay site between Ca Mau and Bac Lieu. We also visited Dong Tam, home base of the 9th Infantry Division, which was supported by Company B of the 52nd Signal Battalion. Dong Tam, seemingly carved out of pure dust, was a bleak, dangerous place. Two Company B signalmen had been killed in a roadside ambush near there during the Tet offensive of 1968.

As Tet 1969 approached, the U.S. Army was busy building up bunkers and defensive positions, in the event the VC tried another big attack as they had during Tet '68. Rumors were circulating that the Viet Cong intended to overrun Can Tho during Tet of 1969.

Very serious in Vietnam, and set to become a first-time company commander.

"Much of the damage from the Tet Offensive of 1968 is still unrepaired. The Vietnamese had been building a new university in Can Tho when the Viet Cong tried to overrun the town," I wrote in late 1968 to my family.

"The VC took over the university building but were driven out by U.S. gunships. The building is a wreck, full of holes," I wrote. "We are still in the midst of a big push and are installing a complete new system of communications," I added.

I felt that I had big shoes to fill in replacing Capt. John McDougle as company commander. He had previous service as a sergeant before going to OCS, and was one of the first to graduate from OCS at Fort Gordon. My background was much flimsier, just high school, and three years of Army experience. I had one of my first encounters with McDougle when I was still assistant S-3 at the battalion headquarters. I had received special orders appointing me as defense counsel in a court martial case.

McDougle had brought desertion charges against one of his men, who was locked up in Long Binh Jail. The jail was often referred to as LBJ, which unfortunately was also the initials of the president at the time, Lyndon Baines Johnson. When McDougle heard that I would be representing the defense, he told me, "Jones, if you get him off, I am going to kick your ass." I laughed it off. McDougle knew as well as me that all defendants get their day in court. This was in the days before the Uniform Code of Military Justice was revised, and non-lawyer officers like me were routinely assigned to handle the defense or prosecution in court martial cases.

It was hardly fair to the defendant.

I traveled to Long Binh Jail to meet with the man I was supposed to represent. He refused to talk to me. In fact, he lay on his back, literally foaming at the mouth. He seemed to be out of his mind. Faced with the dilemma of a defendant who refused to cooperate, I sought advice at the Judge Advocate General's Office. They were stumped, too, but suggested that I try an unorthodox approach and "stand mute." This I did. The court martial board, after a recess during which they did some legal consultation of their own, interpreted the plea as not guilty. The court martial board quickly found my client guilty. Although I had no doubt the man was guilty, I felt badly that I had been unable to do a better job representing him.

No one was happier than me when the Uniform Code of Military Justice was revised, and defendants were guaranteed representation at court martial by a real lawyer.

12 - Command

Soc Trang Army Airfield, 1969. (U.S. Army photo)

Capt. John McDougle passed the company guide-on to me in a brief change-of-command ceremony on Jan. 5, 1969. A dozen or so troops that the sergeants rounded up watched from their formation in front of the tiny company orderly room at Soc Trang Army Airfield. I was now the commander of Company D, which included 120 men, spread over six sites. With this assignment, I became a combat signal unit commander, which would be my primary military occupational speciality (MOS) for the reminder of my active duty days.

At Soc Trang, we had a communications center, a dial telephone exchange, a radio teletype van, and a radio relay and carrier operation. We provided communications support to attack helicopter companies, MACV advisors, Special Forces, better known as Green Berets, engineers, and even an Air Force lieutenant who served as post weather officer. McDougle spent the rest of the day with me, and then we went to the officer's club and shared drinks into the night. The next day, McDougle reported to Can Tho to take a staff position at battalion headquarters. I was told that there had been no enemy activity in the Soc Trang area for several months. Ironically, my very first night there was a mortar attack on the airfield, but there were no casualties and little damage.

It was the first time I heard the sound of an incoming mortar explosion. I came out of my hootch — my room in the officers barracks — and saw that there had been no harm done. I went back to bed. When there was an attack at Soc Trang, it tended to be a hit-and-run affair. The low, flat terrain offered little cover for any enemy looking to make a ground attack. On two sides of the oblong-shaped airfield, constructed by the occupying Japanese during World War II as a fighter base, were rice paddies as far as the eye could see. The narrow entrance of the airfield

Lt. Col. Gerald R. Jennings (standing), was just 31 years old when he served as the battalion commander of the 52nd Signal Battalion. All of his company commanders, kneeling, were first lieutenants. The sergeant major is kneeling in front of Jennings. That's me at right. (U.S. Army Photo)

faced out onto the village of Soc Trang. But the fourth side was a stretch of woods nicknamed the "Tigers Tail" that could spell trouble. It offered cover to the enemy. Pilots occasionally reported taking fire from the Tigers Tail while landing or taking off.

The "Tiger" name came from the fact that one of the aviation units once had a live tiger mascot at Soc Trang. The tiger was gone by the time I arrived, but I have seen video of it, and of GI's roughhousing with the big cat. Tigers aside there was safety in Soc Trang during the day, but at night the village was under lockdown against Viet Cong attack. We couldn't see them, but we knew that the enemy was never far away.

Helping to keep the VC at a respectful distance was the great firepower U.S. units had at Soc Trang. There were two attack helicopter companies, the 121st and the 336th, which brought lethal fire power to the battlefield with their mini-guns and rocket launchers. The airfield also hosted a "Birddog" company, which provided single-engine spotter aircraft to direct firepower, an engineer company, and my own Company D, which was one of the smaller units there. In addition, the airfield was ringed by concrete bunkers where guards stood watch at night with M-60 machine guns, night vision scopes, and triggers for Claymore mines, curved side facing out toward the rice paddies. What infantry there was in the area was ARVN, the South Vietnamese army.

In my first few weeks in Company D, I stayed busy getting to know the enlisted men and non-commissioned officers (NCOs) who operated and maintained the signal equipment in Soc Trang, and the outlying sites of Bac Lieu, Gia Rai, Ca Mau, Vi Thanh and Rach Gia. There were two other officers who reported to me, one at Soc Trang, Lt. Carl Tetzner, and one in Bac Lieu, Lt. Dave Watts. I paid particular attention to accounting for more than $3 million (in 1969 dollars) of communications equipment at the six sites for which I was responsible. Today that would work out to about $20 million. The centerpiece of all that equipment was a 400-line dial telephone exchange at Soc Trang, operated by American and Vietnamese switchboard operators. It was the portal through which calls in our portion of the Mekong Delta were patched to the rest of the world.

Among the Vietnamese operators working in the exchange was Tran Kim Cuc. I didn't know her name for a long time. But I couldn't help noticing her whenever I visited the switchboard room. A warm, beautiful smile can be a thing of wonder.

13 - Soc Trang

Our Jeep was hurtling down the rough two-lane road between Soc Trang and Bac Lieu. Steel pots on our heads, flak jackets zipped up, M-16s rifles locked and loaded, our hearts in our throats. We were headed for Bac Lieu. Even at top speed — about 60 mph, the 30 miles between Bac Lieu and Soc Trang seemed to

First Sgt. Roy Yonemura, right, and I pose next to the Company D sign outside the company orderly room in Soc Trang. The stacked barrels behind Yonemura were filled with earth as a blast barrier.

take forever. We were all alone in a flat, alien vastness of green rice fields, where an enemy might rise up out of a roadside ditch with RPG rockets or AK-47, or set off an explosive charge. There were no other Americans in sight. Just the four men in our Jeep.

Our only contact with friendlies was a Jeep-mounted radio. Soon after taking command of Company D, I begin visiting the unit's five other signal sites. If I needed to get somewhere and a seat wasn't available on a helicopter, we would call air field operations and let them know where we were headed, all by our lonesome, in a Jeep.

On this day, we were headed to Bac Lieu where we had 40 men stationed at a signal site, supporting local American and Vietnamese units with communications.

I was determined not to hunker down in the company headquarters. I needed to be in the field with our men as much as possible. There were hundreds of details to attend to, that could

Even though I was able to wear a baseball cap in garrison at Soc Trang, my helmet was always close by.

not be handled sitting in the orderly room. Were our solders safe? How was morale? Were there any issues? Any troublemakers? And there was more. Were communications security orders getting to where they needed to be? What was the status of a 400-cycle generator Bac Lieu needed? Were we short of any flak jackets or protective masks? Did weapon serial numbers match what was on the inventory? Commanders had been relieved for failing to maintain control of unit weapons.

Fortunately, we never had an ambush, or any other kind of attack on those wild rides through the countryside. But that didn't mean that the enemy wasn't nearby. About week after I was reassigned from Can Tho to Soc Trang, the Can Tho airfield was rocked by a nighttime enemy attack. Viet Cong sappers breeched the defensive positions at Can Tho Airfield — came in through the razor wire — throwing charges into bunkers, killing several American defenders, and destroying aircraft before being killed or driven off. Even though there had been persistent rumors that an attack was coming at Can Tho, it was a shock that the airfield had actually been hit. In the five months I had been assigned to Can Tho, there had been no such attack, only rumors of a possible attack. Soc Trang would not be immune from communist attacks.

July 1969: Awarding a Purple Heart to one of the company signalmen wounded in an enemy mortar attack. Looking on at right is Capt. J. W. Anderson, who replaced me as company commander.

One attack wounded two Company D soldiers who were standing guard on the perimeter on top of their bunker. A mortar round fell behind the bunker and exploded, spraying our signalmen with shrapnel. One of the soldiers was quickly returned to duty, but the other had to be medically evacuated to Japan. Spec. 5 Barry Street, who was the sergeant of the guard the night, was just putting on his flak jacket and steel pot and preparing to return to the perimeter to check on our two bunkers when that mortar round hit. If he had been out there a few minutes sooner, he, too, might have been wounded or killed. Our higher headquarters appointed a lieutenant colonel to investigate the attack. The investigator concluded that the men might have escaped injury had they been inside the bunker, rather than being on top of it behind a row of sandbags. No argument there, although the reason they were on top of the bunker was to get a better view of the terrain in front of the perimeter and to escape the heat and mosquitoes. Inside the bunker, their view was restricted to a slit facing out onto very dark rice fields.

In all likelihood, it was a lucky shot by the Viet Cong, who fired and moved on. If they had adjusted their aim just a little, they might have hit a nearby barracks full of sleeping men.

Soc Trang Air Field was long and narrow, so if the enemy was able to fire a rocket or mortar anywhere inside the perimeter, it would probably hit people or equipment.

One night I heard a loud explosion and came out of my quarters to see a large fireball leaping high into the air on the far side of the runway. VC gunners had hit the fuel dump, and the blaze burned brightly into the night. The impact was maybe about 100 yards away.

Aside from the two men wounded in the mortar attack, the only other casualty we suffered was during an accident. One of our

Just as I frequently visited Company D's signs sites,
I would occasionally receive a visit in Soc Trang

soldiers had gotten hold of an unauthorized "grease gun," an M-3 submachine gun, which dated back to World War II and fired .45 caliber rounds. He accidentally shot himself in the leg.

***

To get to the outlying sites, there were only two ways to travel -- by Jeep or helicopter, or sometimes aboard a C-123 Provider cargo aircraft. The C-123s had two propeller engines, and two jet assists to help it get quickly off the ground. The acceleration was a thrill, but when the pilot cut the jet assist, there was almost a sensation of floating, a total loss of momentum.

The company commanders of the 52nd Signal Battalion pose with the battalion C.O. Lt. Don R. Wong, front center, along the Bassac River in Can Tho. I am, at right in the back row. (U.S. Army Photo)

It would take me about three days to make the circuit of all six sites. Helicopter was the preferred method of travel. With numerous flights in and out of Soc Trang throughout the day, and it was easy enough to wait on the flight line for a departing chopper and to find out if they had an open seat.

One time I flew into our site at Vi Thanh, arriving at a landing strip made out of pierced steel planking, near a canal and a long row of coconut trees. It was out in the middle of nowhere with no sign of a village or people. Finally, I saw a group of ARVN infantry returning from an operation with a stretcher.

When they got a little closer, a distraught American sergeant was crying, saying he had warned his captain, an American advisor, not to go into the operational area. It was too hot.

The group had walked into an ambush. I watched as the body of the young advisor was placed in a body bag. He had a wedding ring on his finger. It was a profoundly sad scene. I couldn't help but grieve for his family and the bad news that would be coming their way.

***

Lt. Col. Don R. Wong, the battalion commander, left, promoted me to captain on May 15, 1969, in the battalion headquarters in Can Tho. (U.S. Army photo)

If there was a hall of fame for Army first sergeants, Roy Yonemura would be in it.

Yonemura, a Japanese-American from Hawaii, was my first sergeant. As a first-time company commander, I found Roy to be invaluable in helping keep the company on an even keel, while I got my footing. First sergeants take care of thousands of details from morning reports to helping keep the noncommissioned officers and enlisted men in line. I had the silver bar of a first lieutenant, command of the company, and all of three years of active duty. Yonemura had more than 20 years of Army experience, and vast knowledge.

"Top," as all first sergeants are called, treated me with respect and concern. Any first-time company commander should be so lucky to have a Roy Yonemura.

Barry Street, one of the up-and coming young NCOs in the company, later reflected, Yonemura "was a good leader and mentor to his troops. He made everyone toe the line but he was fair and respected his troops." Unfortunately, I would lose Roy a couple of months later when he completed his tour. I also lost operations sergeant Glenn Baker, who had to be medically evacuated. Another effective NCO was Staff Sgt. Roger T. Roe, who had a talent for speaking his mind regardless of the consequences. I would re-connect years later with Street and Roe, long after we had all left the service.

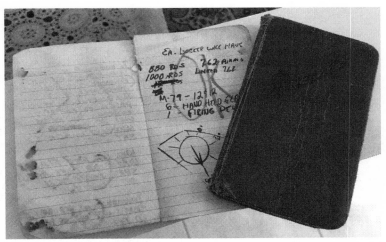

I still have a couple of the little green notebooks I carried in my jungle fatigues during my time as company commander in Vietnam.

Roe's sometimes blunt remarks were offset by his knowledge of communications, and his willingness to work hard and get his hands dirty. I'll never forget coming out of the orderly room one

70

day and seeing the stout figure of Roe, standing fearlessly 100 feet above the ground inside a communication tower whose diameter was not much larger than his girth. Years later, Roe would tell me that the NCOs had a meeting shortly after I had taken command of Company D and decided that even though I was young, I was a quick enough study. They decided to give me the benefit of a doubt and their support.

***

I kept a series of little green Army notebooks with my to-do lists. Among the tasks were rebuilding fighting sites at Vi Thanh which lately had taken incoming fire during the daytime, as well as pouring a concrete generator pad, and moving a mobile communications van. In addition to maintaining communications, we always had concern about enemy activity. Defending our positions was top of mind. I reminded our troops that ammunition must be stored in a central location and no one was allowed to move around the garrison with live ammo. Also, our signalmen would fight as infantry in the event of an attack. They would go to the perimeter if there was a ground attack. One time there was a shell hole in a 200-pair cable near the perimeter. I reported it to the airfield defense commander. He suspected it was from friendly fire and promised it wouldn't happen again.

A few months after being named company commander, I was promoted to captain. Lt. Col. Don R. Wong had replaced Lt. Col. Gerald R. Jennings as battalion commander, after Jennings had been reassigned to 1st Signal Brigade headquarters. Wong, who pinned on my bars as captain, was a no-nonsense officer who personally evaluated each of his company commanders within 30 days of taking command. He tolerated no profanity, no overgrown mustaches, and insisted that the troops understand their MOS, their military occupational speciality — their job.

I was happy to share the news of my promotion with my family. But whatever danger there might be, or any chances that I took, I kept out of my letters. I did not want to alarm anyone.

14 – Her world

*Kim, a switchboard operator in Soc Trang would come
to mean become so much more to me.*

Was I careful about what I wrote in letters to my family back
home? Very careful. I didn't want to worry them. The letters were
so lacking in drama and heroics that they were boring. That's the
way I wanted it. I didn't tell them about Kim, either. Not that there
was much to tell for most of my time in Soc Trang. Sure, Kim, a
switchboard operator for the U.S. Amy, caught my eye right away.
How could she not? Achingly beautiful, with a warm, sweet smile
that lit up the room. Glorious high cheeks, slender, graceful neck
framed by hair that fell sinuously to her shoulders. Demurely and
neatly turned out, she was tall for a Vietnamese woman in 1969 at
5-foot-4, weighing just 95 pounds. Yes, there were many beautiful
women in Vietnam. Not that I was in the market for a girlfriend or
a wife. So why Kim? Who can say what attracts one person to
another? I think with Kim it was her kind personality, her decency,

her intelligence, her professionalism, and her courage. Maybe there was a hint of mystery, too. But whenever I stopped by the switchboard, it was all business. When a caller got Soc Trang 9 on the line, they knew their call would get through, even if they didn't know it was Kim.

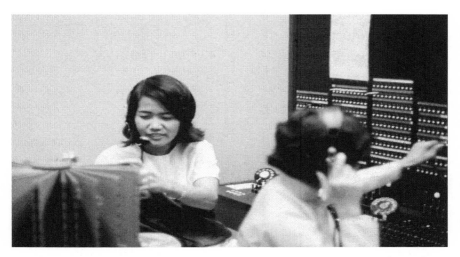

Kim, left, at work in the Soc Trang dial telephone exchange. She didn't know it but I was about to complicate her world.

Kim was so good at her work that the soldiers she worked with nicknamed her "Sgt. Daisy," which made the other switchboard operators a little envious. But despite the respect she earned in the workplace, getting to work was another story. She had to walk past the Vietnamese army guards outside the gates of the airfield. She learned to ignore the taunts and insults hurled at the women who worked for their American Allies. Kim seemed to instinctively know how to navigate the dangerous, treacherous world she had been born into. It was a world where even the Vietnamese might have a hard time knowing who friend was and who was foe. In normal life, a guy sees a girl, likes what he sees, gets to know her, and maybe eventually works up the nerve to ask her out. Let's have coffee. Want to see a movie? With Kim, it would never be that simple. There were none of those dating venues in Vietnam, and there were rules against fraternization. Then one day in April 1969, the NCOs at Soc Trang had a steak cookout and invited me. When I arrived, some of the switchboard operators were there, too. Among them, Kim. I finally had a chance to talk to her outside of her workplace. At first it was just small talk. I worked up the courage to ask her if she was married. The answer was no. She didn't have a boyfriend, either. Good news, because I was interested, and I didn't have anyone either. That's how the relationship started. Very slowly and cautiously.

Sometimes the famous Humphrey Bogart line from Casablanca about all the gin joints in the world comes to mind. Except in this case, I wasn't walking into a gin joint. I was walking into Kim's world, shaking up the order of things.

Life would never be the same for either of us.

Kim and I were both communicators working for the U.S. Army in Vietnam. She was very good at what she did.

15 - Kim

She was a woman in bloom. Blooming against all odds amidst the ugliness, the chaos and the cruelty of war. I would see her walking to work, past the company orderly room to the dial telephone exchange next door where she worked. She was a vision: walking gracefully, almost seeming to float, her pocketbook looped over one shoulder, and her ao dai billowing in the breeze. Kim was the classic Vietnamese beauty, demure, sweet, and possessed of a stubborn will of iron.

If she saw me, she would turn and gift me with a smile.

"Hi Dai Uy," she might say, calling me by my military rank (captain) in Vietnamese.

Kim at a park in downtown Soc Trang.

Whether seated in front of a dial telephone console, or walking to work, she intrigued me with her beauty, with her brightness, and her personality. She seemed to manage the world around her effortlessly, almost as with a hand tied behind her back. Kim was special and I knew it.

With just weeks left before I left Vietnam, I knew I wanted to marry Kim. Not that I had told her so. I knew it in my heart and in

75

my head, and after many debates with myself, I went down to the Soc Trang Post Exchange and bought a diamond engagement ring.

Some love affairs strike like lightning. Others take more time. I didn't have time. I had orders to report to the communications department of the Armor school at Fort Knox where I was scheduled to become an instructor. Fortunately for me, even though we were moving fast, I knew the decision to pursue Kim was the right one. Standing in the way: prejudice, a war, a mountain of red tape, the cultural divide and a language barrier. She was Buddhist, I was Baptist. None of that mattered.

Finding love in the most unexpected place for both of us.

It was an unlikely romance. Kim knew nothing of baseball, The Beatles or the Stones. No part of her universe included Friday night football games, pizza, or the Fourth of July. She hadn't a clue about what American youth or their exasperated parents were concerned about: the draft, the war, and the cultural divide that had torn society so badly. The only Americans that Kim knew in 1969 were those in uniform, like me, soldiers serving far from home, just hoping to survive and get on with their lives. Did she ever hear those stormy echoes from the impossibly distant United States? Where many youth grew their hair, marched in the streets, removed their bras, and burned their draft cards? Maybe, but Kim had more immediate concerns. Her reality was so much harsher than any college student in Gainesville or Berkeley could imagine. She worked to support her 4-year-old son, and to help her family stay alive in the midst of a brutal war. As a Vietnamese woman working for the U.S. Army, she surely faced the danger of being killed by the Viet Cong, or having her family kidnapped or murdered.

For my part, I knew little of a thousand years of Vietnamese struggle. I failed to understand why Vietnamese soap operas were so obsessed with despair and grief. I knew almost nothing of the language, and little of a diet which seemed to be all about rice and fish sauce. And those chop sticks! I knew about forks, and knives and spoons. I wondered how anyone could get food into their mouth with chop sticks. To be honest, I knew little about Kim herself. But somehow, I knew what mattered. I knew her heart.

I vowed to do whatever was necessary to marry Kim and bring her back to the United States. Nobody said it would be easy. As we got to know each other, I quickly learned that she was unafraid to speak her mind. She would be true to herself. She was no pushover.

One day we were having a quarrel. Kim in a flowing Vietnamese dress, and me, a U.S. Army captain in jungle fatigues. We were standing off the dusty main road outside her house in Soc Trang, deep in Vietnam's Mekong Delta. As always, the midday sun was blistering, and the gritty, red sand was blowing in the wind. We were oblivious to the chaos swirling around us, the rice farmers, soldiers, and shopkeepers, walking past, and the bicycles competing with 2 1/2-ton Army trucks for a share of the road. For a few moments, we even forgot about the bloody Vietnam War. My focus narrowed to Kim. I told her how much I loved her. I remembered something in my pocket. I fished out a diamond ring that I had just bought in the post exchange and said just about the only Vietnamese words that I knew: "Anh yeu em" (I love you). And in English, I asked, "Would you marry me?" Kim seemed shocked; the surprise written across her face. She took a step backward. But after a short pause, she composed herself, and said, "Yes." I placed the ring on her finger and kissed her. The argument was forgotten.

16 - Numbers

By custom in Vietnam, the first-born child is referred to as "Number two." The second-born is "Number-Three," and so on. Nobody gets to be number-one. Kim was the first-born in her family. Her younger brothers and sisters called her Chi, pronounced "J," or Chi Hai, sister number-two. As the oldest child of six who survived into adulthood, she shared child-rearing duties.

Kim shows a mix of mystery and inquisitiveness in this photo.

While still a little girl, she carried a younger brother or sister on her hip, while her parents worked in the rice fields. When Kim was a little older, she would join her parents in the rice fields, or sell home-made snacks and treats near the house. Her parents were firm, strict and upright. They treated neighbors with kindness and helpfulness. Kim's father used water buffalo for plowing and made mosquito nets to protect them at night. During the celebration of the lunar new year, he would give each of the animals a beer.

The Tran and Lieu families, Kim's paternal and maternal sides, had been in Bac Lieu at least since the 1800s. The family was

Buddhist, and helped start two local temples, the oldest in 1876. The Tran family, and all Vietnamese, remembered the French who had colonized their country, and the Japanese who had imposed their "Greater East Asia Co-Prosperity Sphere," what they were calling Asia for Asians. In truth, the Vietnamese didn't like being occupied by the Japanese any more than they had the French. After World War II, the French attempted to resume control of Indochina, but were met by the Vietminh, under the leadership of Ho Chi Minh. Vietnam did not win its independence until 1954 with the French defeat at Dien Bien Phu. Elections failed to materialize, and the country was split into the communist north and the nationalist south.

When Kim was an elementary school student, one of her classes was French, taught by a schoolteacher aunt. Kim also learned a little of Chinese from her mother. Starting in the early 1960s, war became a way of life, with the Viet Cong secretly recruiting young men and women throughout Vietnam, assassinating village chiefs and trying to destabilize the south. That was the world that Kim was born into, and while she might have wished otherwise, she went about her life the best she could as she grew to become a young woman. It was only normal for her to know the location of the nearest bunker, and if she was at home, there would be one right under her roof. A wise person did not venture out at night, out of respect for the curfew, and out of caution for what else might be out there.

When Kim got old enough, she became a Buddhist nun. She might have stayed in the temple for the rest of her life, as some of her friends did, but felt the need to financially help her family. When the Americans entered Vietnam, she went to night school to learn English. She got a job at Soc Trang Army Airfield and was recruited to become a switchboard operator. And that's where I first knew Kim by yet another number, Soc Trang 9.

17 – A promise

I had a lot of questions.

Kim and her friend Bich Tu, right. Both women were switchboard operators for the U.S. Army in Soc Trang.

But for now, I was going on faith, the belief that with enough determination Kim and I would be able to get married and have a life together in the United States. I thought I would extend my tour of duty in Vietnam to buy the time to get the Army's permission to marry. When I saw the personnel officer of the 52nd Signal Battalion in July 1969, I told him what I wanted to do. Impossible, the warrant officer said.

"Sir, you already have your orders to Fort Knox, Ky., and you're leaving Vietnam," he said.

I should have requested an extension earlier. But things were moving too fast, and I didn't know any better. The Army may move on its belly, but it also moves on paper. It was too late to get an extension of time. But the personnel officer who was adamant that I couldn't stay in Vietnam also offered a possible solution. I could return to the United States, and report to the Department of the Army in Washington, D.C., while on leave, and request reassignment to Vietnam, he said.

It was a long way to travel to get back to where I already was. But that was my only option.

I gave Kim the news, along with my phone number and address in St. Augustine, Fla., where I would be on leave.

"Call me when you can. But know that I'm coming back," I said.

The 400-line dial telephone exchange at Soc Trang was where Kim worked. Barrels filled with earth were stacked around the building as shield against rocket or mortar attack.

As the truck carrying me to the landing field at Soc Trang for the flight to Tan Son Nhut Air Force Base pulled away, I caught a glimpse of Kim's face. I will never forget the look of quiet sadness and dignity. My promise to return probably sounded hollow to anyone in Soc Trang who heard about it. How many times have girlfriends been jilted? Kim's Vietnamese friends and the American G.I.s all told her that I would never be back. She would calmly answer, "That's OK."

I left Vietnam in July 1969, the same month that John Lennon and The Beatles released "Give Peace a Chance." I arrived back in the United States to find my family glued to the TV. Neil Armstrong was walking on the moon. I wondered how one nation was able to fight a war in Southeast Asia, while putting a man on the lunar surface. The tip-off to my family that something was afoot came when Kim called me in St. Augustine while I was on leave and Margie, my stepmother, took the call. Margie handed me the phone and hovered nearby, listening while I talked to Kim. The secret was out. I would have to tell my family about my plans before I was ready. I broke the news to them as gently as possible.

"I'm going back to Vietnam, and I am going to marry Kim. She is wonderful. You'll love her," I said. Nobody tried to talk me out of my plans. But I could see they were worried. I traveled to Washington, D.C., and got approval to return to Vietnam. The Army even gave me my choice of assignments. I requested 1st Signal Brigade, knowing that Long Binh was one of the largest Army installations in the world. It would be the ideal place to tackle all that red-tape, whatever it entailed. At this point I really didn't know what would be involved.

Despite the dangers, I had no hesitation about returning to a place that so many tried to avoid. That didn't make me brave. Just willing to pursue my destiny, and the woman I loved. I couldn't imagine living without her, even though that was a very real possibility.

18 - Reunion

When I returned to Vietnam in September of 1969, the first thing I did was find a phone in Long Binh and call Soc Trang to let Kim know that I was back.

For the love of this woman, I was back in Vietnam in September 1969, surprising more than a few people who thought the promise of my return was just empty talk.

I was elated to be back in Vietnam. It also was a vindication for Kim and her faith in me. After I settled in at Long Binh, I began to familiarize myself with my new assignment as "buddy project officer" at 1st Signal Brigade. It was a part of the effort to "Vietnamize the war," and it would take me a few weeks to get back to Soc Trang to visit Kim. Soc Trang was about 160 miles south of Long Binh, and it was not an easy trip to make. I took a military bus from Long Binh to Saigon's Tan Son Nhut Air Force Base, and then waited for a flight that was heading south.

Soon enough, the American senior advisor from Can Tho, a major general, arrived with his staff in dress uniform aboard a fixed wing aircraft. They changed planes and boarded a jetliner for a trip to the United States. I checked with the pilot of the senior advisor's aircraft, and found out that there was an open seat. I was invited aboard for the flight back to Can Tho.

Once at Can Tho, I caught a ride on a helicopter to Soc Trang Airfield. I reported to the orderly room of Company D, and Capt. J. W. Anderson, who had replaced me in July, gave me a ride to Kim's house. It was an emotional, joyous reunion having Kim back in my arms again. Anderson was supposed to have dinner with us the next day, but there was trouble in the company, and he had to take a man to Long Binh Jail.

***

In my first few months back in Vietnam, I saw little of Kim. She was too far away.

I urged her to leave her job in Soc Trang, and move to Saigon.

Three good friends: Kim, left, Chin, third from left, and Hanh, far right.

That was perhaps my first major request of her -- to leave a job she enjoyed, and more significantly, to move away from her family. Until we could move her closer, there were frequent phone calls, and notes. In one she asked the eternal question, "Will you still love me when I am old?"

In early 1970, Kim gave up her job in Soc Trang and moved to Saigon, where a friend from Soc Trang, named Hanh, helped her find a small, cold-water apartment. It was a lonely time for Kim, in that apartment, alone most of the time while I worked in Long Binh. But a few weeks later, Hanh, who was now living with her then-boyfriend, Fred Freund, invited Kim to share a two-story house with them in the Saigon's Gia Dinh district. I knew Hanh casually from Soc Trang, when she worked in the post exchange.

I didn't know Fred at all, and frankly didn't trust this fellow in civilian clothes who spoke English with a German accent. Soon enough, however, I learned that Fred worked for IBM and was a contractor for Military Assistance Command, Vietnam. Fred helped MACV keep track of all the statistics that Defense Secretary Robert McNamara and others would often quote. When Kim told me that she could rent a room from Fred and Hanh, I agreed this was good news. It would make her time in Saigon more pleasant and less isolated. Fred turned out to be a decent guy, and something of a character. He was funny, brash, and opinionated. He was unafraid to banter with Saigon taxi drivers, or haggle with the street merchants. Fred and Hanh were very kind to Kim and me.

In 1970, I met two of Kim's other friends, Jeff and Chin Klein, in Saigon as they were preparing to leave Vietnam for Baltimore, Md.

Kim after the move to Saigon.

Jeff Klein was from Baltimore, and could have been one of the teen characters in the classic movie "Diner." Jeff had met Chin in Soc Trang, when he served as company clerk at the 121st Aviation Company. Jeff

85

returned to the United States after completing his military service, and then came back to Vietnam as a civilian, selling new cars to G.I.'s through the PX. But the real reason he was back in Vietnam was Chin. Jeff liked to tell the story of visiting Kim in Soc Trang, and how she served him a Coca-Cola. It was a small gesture, but Jeff never forgot the hospitality and spirit of sharing from someone who had so little. Years later when I saw the movie "Joy Luck Club," I thought that could be the story of Kim and her friends Hanh and Chin. They shared all of their joys and aspirations and their heartbreaks, too. We saw Chin and Jeff just as they were leaving Vietnam in 1970 for Baltimore.

Things were a lot more uncertain for Kim and me, and for Hanh and Fred. The U.S. involvement in Vietnam was winding down, and troop strength which once exceeded half a million was being rapidly reduced. In November 1970, the Stars and Stripes newspaper reported that the U.S. Army had turned over Soc Trang Airfield to the South Vietnamese army.

"The American flag was lowered for the last time over Soc Trang airfield Wednesday during a ceremony in which Robert C. Seamans Jr., secretary of the Air Force, helped mark the first transfer of a totally American-run base to the Vietnamese," Larry McQuillan, an S&S staff correspondent, reported.

The two American helicopter companies based at Soc Trang, the 121st and the 336th, were inactivated, and their helicopters turned over to the Vietnamese. Among those attending the ceremony was Gen. Creighton W. Abrams, commander of MACV. The only thing that was certain was that Kim and I no longer had all the time in the world.

Her move to Saigon would not only bring us closer but would help us in the task of pulling together the official paperwork we needed to get married, as well as submitting to counseling and background investigations.

19 - Vietnamization

For my second tour in Vietnam, I would be part of the 18,000-strong 1st Signal Brigade, headquartered in Long Binh. I was a member of a team working on the "Vietnamization" of the communications network. Working with our Vietnamese counterparts was dubbed "Buddies Together." The 1st Signal Brigade was massive -- larger than any U.S. division -- and provided communications support to U.S. forces in Vietnam and Thailand.

The Buddy program – Cung Than-Thien -- was designed to train Vietnamese communicators to take over the then-state-of-the-art backbone system, with the unwieldy title of Integrated Communications System - Southeast Asia, and the dial telephone exchanges. It was a system that handled 8 million messages a month and was the most sophisticated Army communications system in history. We were training the Vietnamese to be technical controllers, to repair microwave systems and fixed

Capt. James A. Jones Jr., Buddy Officer

plant carrier equipment, and to operate and maintain dial central offices.

To deal with the language barrier, the 1st Signal Brigade opted to first train the Vietnamese communicators in English, before moving on to the technical training.

"An understanding of English was necessary since the system would be used jointly by the United States and South Vietnam before it was turned over completely to South Vietnam," said the charismatic commander of the 1st Signal Brigade, Major General Thomas Rienzi, in his final report before leaving Vietnam in 1970.

"The language problem has been present throughout our experience in Vietnam and has never been really solved," Rienzi said. The training took place at the Republic of Vietnam Armed Forces signal training facility in Vung Tau, a seaside resort. Once the Vietnamese communicators completed their classroom training, they were placed at communications sites and dial telephone exchanges throughout South Vietnam. When they were deemed "site qualified," they would replace their U.S. counterparts. The newly qualified Vietnamese signalmen would return to their parent units and instruct others.

Richard Nixon, who had beaten Hubert Humphrey in the 1968 presidential election, said "The rate of American withdrawals depend on three criteria - progress in the training of the South Vietnamese, progress in the Paris negotiations and the level of enemy activity." Obviously, the 1st Signal Brigade's part of the bargain was the training. Other elements of the Buddy project included refresher training and training in soft-skill areas, such as cable splicing, at the U.S. Army's signal school in Long Binh. In addition, the Buddy program encouraged an exchange of staff visits, the exchange of awards and decorations, and social get-togethers between Americans and the Vietnamese. The aim was to make the South Vietnamese forces self-reliant, in Vietnamese, "ba tu."

The training division at 1st Signal Brigade actually had two focuses: the Buddy project, and the training of U.S. communicators. After 1969, the Buddy project grew increasingly important. As a staff officer, it was my job to help with the reports, the briefings, the staff coordination, the staff visits and the various training programs. Then, as now, training was a never ending process. Many American G.I.s received additional training at Long Binh. A much needed skill was cable splicing because so much cable was exposed to gunfire. We also provided feedback to the stateside schools on the need to add two weeks to the radio carrier course for trouble shooting.

Major Daniel L. Hudson was my direct supervisor. We became close friends. Dan, a native West Virginian, was a Regular Army officer whose most recent assignment had been in the U.S. Embassy in Montevideo,

Uruguay. He and his wife, Linda, had a baby girl named Terri. Dan was a very bright and personable guy who knew how to navigate the bureaucratic channels of a large command like the 1st Signal Brigade. We worked hard on the job, and the friendship grew strong. He knew that I was trying to pull together the paperwork the Army said that I needed to marry a Vietnamese national. He was sympathetic and supportive of my struggle. I wanted Dan to be my best man at the wedding, but I still hadn't worked my way through all the red tape before his tour of duty ended and he left for his next assignment in the United States.

That was another disappointment. But our problems were nothing compared to the tragedy of the Vietnam War. To quote Humphrey Bogart in Casablanca: "It doesn't take much to see that the problems of three little people don't amount to a hill of beans in this crazy world."

20 – Our turn

There were consequences for a U.S. soldier who wanted to marry a Vietnamese woman. During the Vietnam War, the possible hazards and pitfalls were enormous. I started the process Sept. 19, 1969, by signing this statement:

"I, James A. Jones Jr., understand the ramifications involved in my proposed marriage to a non-U.S. citizen, in that if derogatory information is found in the security check of my intended spouse, I am subject to loss of my security clearance and possible removal from the country within 24 hours, if authorities deem my position sensitive enough to warrant the above action."

Obviously, my military career, such as it was, was on the line. That was just the start of the process, which would include mandatory counseling by a chaplain, an Army lawyer, medical clearance for Miss Kim and me, and the security check. In all, the application which was finally completed and submitted June 20, 1970, had 21 enclosures.

Eleven months after we had started the paperwork, we received permission from Military Assistance Command Vietnam to get married. The letter was dated Aug. 29, 1970. The background checks, the counseling, and all the other paperwork in a one-inch thick packet had turned up no reason why we shouldn't marry. But we couldn't marry right away. We would have to wait until Nov. 3, 1970, which was five months before my projected departure from Vietnam. That was the rule.

"While the laws of Vietnam require only a civil ceremony, you are encouraged to have a religious ceremony performed by a chaplain or minister of the appropriate faith," the letter of approval said.

The letter also advised that the U.S. government would not be authorized to offer transportation to the United States for Kim. That would be up to me. Finally, we should report to the U.S. Counselor Section for assistance in getting a Vietnamese passport for Kim's immigration to the U.S. It was a good day, and a relief after investing so much time, energy and worry in the quest to get married. On Dec. 8, 1970, we obtained a marriage certificate from the village hall at Hiep-Hoa, near Bien Hoa. It was now an official marriage, but there had been no ceremony. Somehow, we found marriage invitations and sent them to the 1st Signal Brigade staff members. The date for the wedding service at Long Binh Chapel was Dec. 11, 1970. Fred Freund would bring Kim and her friend, Hanh, the bride's maid, to Long Binh in an IBM company car.

The chapel filled up. We waited. We waited some more. Then came the realization: something had gone wrong. Kim, Fred and Hanh were not coming to the wedding. It felt like the universe had collapsed onto me. I was angry, fearful, and frustrated. After about an hour, the chapel began to empty. I had no explanation to offer the chaplain and the departing guests.

"I'll find out tonight when I go to Saigon," I told them.

All of the reasons I could imagine for Kim being a no show were bad. I was afraid for her, and for myself. Had there been an accident? Had Kim decided not to marry me? There was no way that I could call Kim – there was no phone in the house where she was staying in Saigon. There was no way that I could send anyone to check on her. My only option was to travel to Saigon that night after work and investigate myself. When I arrived in Saigon at Fred's house, I was relieved to find everyone unharmed and safe.

She signed her name Tran Kim Cuc for the last time Dec. 14, 1970.
Now she was Cuc Kim Jones.

"We were stopped by the Saigon police with Kim and the bridal cake on the way to the wedding," Fred explained.

Unknown to Fred, the IBM car he was driving had been in an accident with one of his co-workers at the wheel, and the Saigon police were looking for it. Yes, a Viet Cong might pass anonymously through the streets of Saigon, but an American car stood out glaringly in those days.

"The car was impounded and you had to send a military rescue team to transport us to the delayed wedding," Fred would later say.

Fred, a fellow who was quick on his feet, and who had survived the Holocaust, was unable to persuade the police to release the wedding party. He even offered to surrender his identification papers to them but was refused. The memory of the incident remains almost too difficult for Kim to talk about.

"Just miserable. Disappointed," she would say later of that day. "We waited hours in the police station. Everything was ruined – the flowers, the cake," she said. "We took the cake home and shared it with neighbors," Kim said. I was disappointed, too, but relieved. This was the best outcome of any that I might have imagined.

A spontaneous moment at our wedding: Kim ducks away from a kiss. In her culture, public displays of affection were frowned upon.

We decided to reschedule the wedding in three days, to Dec. 14, and this time I would drive a Jeep down from Long Binh to pick up the wedding party in Saigon. I would be a one-man "rescue team."

"That's it, no more stopping," Kim said of the ride to Long Binh in an Army Jeep.

It must have been some sight: me in my jungle fatigues, driving the Jeep, Kim in the passenger seat in her white bridal gown and veil, and in the back seat, Fred in his civilian suit, and Hanh in her traditional Vietnamese long dress. Who knows what went through the military policeman's mind when we reached the main gate at Long Binh.

"We're going to get married," I said, exchanging salutes with the MP at the gate.

We drove to my BOQ, where I changed out of my jungle fatigues, and got into my dress khakis, and then drove on to Long Binh Chapel. When we arrived, all the pews were full. The guests who had waited at the chapel three days earlier when Kim was a no-show, returned. Kim was radiant in a white gown and veil with a spray of flowers on one arm. She was nervous, too, standing in front of a sanctuary filled with American GIs in jungle fatigues. Chaplain Norman Brown, sweating heavily in his pastoral robes in the heat of the chapel, greeted us warmly and got right to work.

After pronouncing us man and wife, Chaplain Norman Brown peeled off his pastoral robes and congratulated Kim. He was drenched in sweat from the tropical heat.

"Dearly beloved, we are gathered together here in the sight of God, and in the face of this company, to join together this man and this woman in holy matrimony," Brown began.

At the conclusion of the service, Brown asked for blessings on the marriage and said that I could kiss the bride. Kim immediately ducked away in embarrassment. But after some coaxing, she finally let me.

"It's not the Vietnamese way," Kim said of that kiss after the wedding. "You couldn't kiss in public back then, you couldn't even hold hands."

94

We returned to the 1st Signal Brigade for a small reception. We were thrilled and could not stop smiling. Afterward, I drove back to my BOQ, changed into my jungle fatigues, and drove Kim, Hanh and Fred back to Saigon, before returning the Jeep to the motor pool in Long Binh. A lot of steps, for sure, but I had orders allowing me to spend seven days of R&R (rest and recuperation) in Saigon. That would be where we spent our honeymoon.

During the honeymoon, we went to a downtown cinema and saw "Guess Who's Coming to Dinner" in French with English and Vietnamese subtitles. It was a three-year old movie about an interracial couple starring Katharine Houghton, Sidney Poitier, Katharine Hepburn, and Spencer Tracy. The couple was in love and bravely facing any potential challenges.

We also had lunch one day on a floating restaurant, the My Canh Café, that had been attacked by the Viet Cong several times. We were just about the only customers that day and ate our lunch in peace. Fortunately, there no grenades thrown at the boathouse. At the time, Kim didn't seem to think too much about the danger of stepping onto that floating restaurant. Years later, she said that knowing what she knows now, she would have been too scared to go there if she had it to do over. With the clarity of hindsight, there might have

From our first Christmas card in 1970: Peace on Earth. Good will

been a few other things we would have done differently. But youth has its own clarity of vision, of certainty, and of, yes, defiance, too. There was no second-guessing whether this marriage was the right thing to do. I knew that it was. For all the ways that we had been tested, I was sure that it would endure.

We were married in Vietnam, the Land of the Dragon, in 1970, the lunar year of the dog. My sign in the Chinese zodiac is the dog. So 1970 really was my year. Christmas was in the air when we got married. I had not been home for the holiday since 1966. But this year I was not alone. We had a Christmas card made with our photo together in Saigon. The message from the Vietnam War was the eternal hope: "Peace on Earth. Good Will Toward Men."

During our honeymoon, we stopped at a monument in Saigon to the nations helping the South Vietnamese in their fight against the Viet Cong. That's Kim in yellow.

21 - Brothers

Altogether, 2.7 million Americans served in Vietnam. Several members of my family — most of them draftees like me — were there, too. I didn't have an accounting of everyone while I was in Vietnam. Some I didn't know about until many years later. I was in touch with my brother-in-law, Jim Presnell, while we were both in Vietnam. He was a helicopter mechanic in Bearcat, a major base east of Saigon. Jim had been a classmate at St. Augustine High School, the best player on the football team, and a shot putter on the track team. He always had a joke, a smile, and a cheery laugh. But there was little that was funny when he wrote me around the time of Tet of 1969, the Year of the Rooster. The massive countrywide offensive by the Viet Cong a year earlier was on everybody's mind.

"We have been either on red or yellow alert, mostly red," Jim wrote me. "The whole company, except the reaction force, mans the green line at night and we work from 7 to 7, seven days a week. It's really warm. I must say I am scared. Charles (GI slang for the Viet Cong) is really showing his butt up here now," Jim wrote.

A few months later, I stopped by Bearcat and visited with Jim, and met his friends, as I was leaving Vietnam after my first tour. They were a bunch of good guys, who made me feel right at home in the enlisted barracks. There were a few beers shared that night. An ex-brother-in-law served with the 2nd Squadron of the 1st Cavalry near Pleiku.

"We were securing the roads and highways for the 4th Infantry Division so they could dash into Cambodia without too much hassle," he wrote me while he was on a week and a half stand-down after humping through the jungle. "The Cav moves around a lot. It seems to me that's all that we do. I believe the reason for that is that during April there was a larger offensive in our area, then right after that the Cambodia thing came up. We're moving again in a few days, but I haven't the slightest idea where we'll be going," he wrote. He added that he had put in for a transfer to another unit.

"I don't like working with tanks and tracks out in the boonies. I know I would feel much better on the ground, because on a vehicle you stick out like a sore thumb and during a firefight that doesn't quite make it," he wrote.

My first-cousin Merritt Jefferson Jones of Durham, N.C., was drafted the same day as me, Feb. 10, 1966. Merritt and I were close, and shared summer memories of roaming and playing on our grandfather's farm in South Boston, Va. We also shared our grandfather's name: Alfred for me, Jefferson for Merritt. Merritt went to Vietnam a year before me, serving aboard an LCM (landing craft mechanized) that cruised Vietnam's brown-water rivers from August 1966 to August 1967.

" You could haul troops or tanks in the well deck," Merritt said. "For about five months we were based in Saigon and used the boat like a tugboat. We would push barges loaded with anything from 500 tons of small arms ammunition to bombs to different places up and down the river. We would also push tanker barges loaded with jet fuel. Then after five months we got sent to the Mekong Delta. There we were attached to an artillery unit. At first they put a 105 howitzer in the well deck. Then we would go out to support the infantry. They would set the coordinates and fire from the boat. But every time they would fire, they would have to reset their coordinates because the big gun would move the boat back, even when we had all four engines running full speed ahead. So then they came up with the idea to use a barge and put two big guns – 105 and 155 – on the barge. They would anchor the barge to the shore and set their coordinates. When they fired, they did not need to change the coordinates. Until you actually see how people live in the world, you do not realize how good we have it in America," Merritt said.

Another first cousin, Mark Johnson, had several tours of duty in Vietnam, including serving as a helicopter crew chief flying out of Soc Trang, but not at the same time as me. All of us would make it out of Vietnam alive. While the public seemed to lose interest in the war, or turn against the continued American presence there, our families remained steadfast in their support of us with letters, tapes, and packages. My mother even got me a subscription to

Playboy. Those letters showed me that life was going on without the men and women in Vietnam. My mother was going through a nasty divorce and two of my sisters, Phyllis, and Sandi, had gotten married since I entered the service.

Sandi, an ardent opponent of the war who took part in peace demonstrations, wrote the most interesting and supportive letters from home. She also gave me a glimpse into a hip counter-culture that I could scarcely relate to as her idols changed from Ringo Starr to Broadway Joe Namath. While still loving The Beatles, she embraced the Doors and Big Brother and the Holding Company as well. Often, Sandi would add a little inscription under her signature. Once it was a sketch of a peace symbol and she added her take on John Lennon's words: "Give it a chance."

Sandi, my peace loving sister.

On another, she wrote: After the verb 'to love,' 'to help 'is the most beautiful verb in the world. Actually, I think those might have been infinitives, rather than verbs, but I agreed with the sentiment.

Sandi also quoted Jonathan Swift: "We have just enough religion to make us hate, but not enough to make us love one another." In one of her letters, Sandi thanked me for answering a question about an Army division. "He really doesn't tell me anything," Sandi said of her husband. "He masks those things from me." I slipped up a little in one of my letters to Sandi when I wrote that his morale seemed a little better than it had been.

"Why would his morale be bad, other than the obvious?" she asked.

Indeed.

Sandi also showed a lot of interest in Kim, as did my mother. Kim got busy having the traditional Vietnamese dress, the ao dai, made for Sandi and my mother, and we mailed them back to the United States. Both had slender builds and could easily wear an ao dai, as we saw when they mailed photos back to us wearing their new dresses.

I took that as a very good sign.

22 –Goodbye, Vietnam

In 1971, I visited I Corps as part of a 1st Signal Brigade inspection team. Shown above is the Citadel at Hue, scene of fierce fighting during the Tet Offensive in 1968.

In early 1971, Kim was trying to cross a Saigon street, when she was knocked down by a hit-and-run motorcyclist, gashing the back of her head. She asked bystanders who came to her aid to take her to the American hospital at Tan Son Nhut, where medics stitched the wound and sent her home. She mended just fine. But it reminded me that anything could happen in Vietnam, much of it bad. I wondered if my luck would continue to hold. I felt that it really was time to leave after spending nearly three years in the war zone. Then in our waning months in Vietnam, I was selected as part of an inspection team to visit signal units close to the demilitarized zone. Among them were Dong Ha, five miles from the DMZ, Quang Tri, Hue and DaNang. It was the first time I had been so far north, with most of my previous time spent in Long Binh and the most southern parts of Vietnam. I gained an appreciation for the troops and units so close to North Vietnam, and the difficulty of their assignment. I was happy to get the job done, and safely return to Long Binh.

Shortly before we were to leave Vietnam, Kim's mother, Lieu Thi Bay brought Kim's son, Phuc, and Kim's little sister Nga, who was the same age as my little sister Carolyn, to visit Saigon. I thought Kim's mother was lovely, but worn looking, not surprising given the immense stresses caused by the war and a lifetime of poverty. Nga was a cute 12-year-old, charming in her little girl innocence. Speaking little Vietnamese, however, all I could do was smile and nod at them.

At the last moment, Kim and her mother decided to keep Phuc in Vietnam. They wanted to make sure that everything in the U.S. would be OK before allowing him to leave the safety of grandma's home. That came as a surprise to me, because we already had the immigration documents we needed for Kim and her son, who we would later give the American name of Dan, to travel to the U.S. I tried to talk her out of it, but they had already decided that Dan, who was much beloved in the family, would stay in Vietnam for a while. Kim had saved enough money to build a home for her mother and father in Bac Lieu, which while modest by American standards, was a big step up from the hut in which they previously lived.

In June of 1971, Kim and I went to Tan Son Nhut Air Force Base to await our flight. Although I was a captain, the Air Force assigned us field grade quarters, normally reserved for majors and colonels, as we stayed over-night on the base. The next morning, we boarded a commercial airliner packed with soldiers, and held our breath until the plane taxied down the runway and lifted off. Only then was I certain that Kim was headed to the U.S. with me. She was probably the only person on that aircraft who didn't cheer as the wheels lifted off the runway.

Kim got her green card when we landed in Honolulu. I could tell she was depressed by all that she was leaving behind and worried about the future. My return to the United States marked the end of four years and three days of overseas service. I was returning to the United States a changed man. From here on, everything would be different for Kim and for me.

We had gotten to know Saigon well between 1969 and 1971, when I made this photo from an overhead walkway near the the Saigon market. I wouldn't see Saigon again until 2006, when it had become a high-rise metropolis and been renamed Ho Chi Minh

23 – The United States

My mother and sisters, Phyllis and Sandi, met us when we arrived in Jacksonville. There were hugs and smiles as we prepared to start a new life in the United States. I was so proud of my new wife and eager to introduce her to my family. The only thing that had gone wrong was that someone had pilfered our luggage and stolen Kim's jewelry. All except for a string of pearls.

Kim experiences snow for the first time in Augusta,

Then it was on to St. Augustine, where Kim would meet my father, my stepmother Margie, and sisters Nancy, Kathy and Carolyn, and my little brother, Tony. I was relieved that everyone embraced Kim, but I shouldn't have been surprised. All the signals I had been receiving from the U.S. pointed to a warm family welcome. After a few weeks in Florida, we drove to Fort Gordon, Ga., and found an apartment in Augusta.

For my new assignment at Fort Gordon, I would be a company commander for several hundred Signal Corps trainees. It wasn't what I had hoped for, given the fact that I had a wife who was brand-new to the U.S. A staff job would have allowed me more time to help her get adjusted.

It would be a bigger adjustment for Kim than I imagined. For the first few months, she would be nervous and fearful when we went for a drive at night. There's not going to be an ambush, or a shakedown at some kind of a military checkpoint, I would tell her. The first time we got on an escalator in a department store, I looked around from the next floor up and saw Kim still at the landing below. She had never before been on an escalator, and like someone on a pair of water skis for the first time, she needed a little coaching.

When I took Kim for her first ride on a roller coaster, she crouched on the floor. I had to hang on to her and the safety bar with all my strength to keep her from being ejected. I could never persuade her that roller coasters were fun and safe. Ironic, considering how many times she had hopped on a helicopter without a second thought during the Vietnam War.

In those days, the food staples that Kim depended on, such as fish sauce, was almost impossible to find except in the rare Asian store. She and other Vietnamese wives at Fort Gordon quickly bonded and established a sisterhood. That helped them weather the huge cultural shift they were experiencing and not feel so alone and isolated. Then there was snow. That first winter we were assigned to Fort Gordon, a winter storm brought 14 inches of snow to an area that hardly ever saw the white stuff. Kim, who had never seen snow, thought it was pretty, but she spent most of her time shivering in our apartment.

***

The long, divisive war in Vietnam had left the Army a wreck after Vietnam. It was rapidly changing, soon becoming an all-volunteer force, and expanding the role of women. In our battalion, two of the four all-male companies were inactivated, and transformed into an all-female outfit.

For a while, there were nuisance nighttime bomb threats to the women's barracks. Some of the male G.I.'s would loiter outside the women's barracks to watch them leave their building in their night clothes. Thankfully, the novelty of having women in the battalion soon wore off. One night, there was an assault outside an on-base movie theater when one trainee slugged another. The victim fell, hitting his head on a curb and died.

The Military Police were getting nowhere with their investigation, so several of us began calling trainees into the battalion headquarters where we quizzed them individually about what they had seen. It was the women who stepped up and gave us the name of the assailant. We called the MPs, and said go pick him up, he's at switchboard operator school. The suspect was court martialed and convicted. He received 20 years imprisonment at Fort Leavenworth and a bad conduct discharge.

Company formation at Fort Gordon. That's me on the left.

At Fort Gordon, I also started my college education. In the daytime I was a company commander and at night I was a college student. That unfortunately left even less time for Kim. But it worked out and we made friends in the battalion and the neighborhood. Kim fit right in wherever we went. And she learned to drive, too. I gave Kim her first driving lesson. But when she came a little close to a building in a parking lot, I lost my nerve and yelled. We quickly agreed that she should enroll in a driving school. Soon enough she had her license and was driving around town and taking her turn during vacation trips.

I took her to our first Christmas party at the Fort Gordon Officers Club. Kim was dazzling in an ao dai, the long flowing Vietnamese dress that was split up the side to the waist and worn over black or white pajama pants. An officer who I didn't know came over and congratulated me on my wife. I was proud of her then, as I am now, not only for her good looks, but for all those other good qualities. Even so, things weren't quite right. She returned to Vietnam in 1973, flying into a very hot war zone, to bring her son Dan back to the U.S. As I was driving home from the airport, "Photograph," a hit song by Ringo Starr and George Harrison, came on the radio. It's a mournful song about lost love. All the guy has left is his memories and a photograph. It was one of those moments when a song perfectly captures the emotion of the moment. In this case, it was foreboding and despair. Anything could go wrong. It was out of my hands. All I could do was go about my business, hoping for the best.

Part of business was communicating with the U.S. Embassy in Saigon to make sure the paperwork was in place to bring Dan back to the United States. Fortunately, after an agonizing few weeks, Kim was headed back to the United States with her son. Her parents and other family members in Vietnam cried when the little boy left with Kim. He was beloved in the family, with a sweet disposition much like Kim's.

"I couldn't look back when we left. I knew that if I saw my mother and father crying it would have been too painful," Kim said.

When Dan, as we would call him, came to the United States with his mother, things were finally as they should be. No longer would he have to hide his mother's pocketbook, to prevent her from leaving. She would never again be apart from this handsome, bright, little boy.

One night I was fiddling with my tape recorder in our Augusta apartment, recording the sound of a rainstorm, and the conversation in the house. There was a clap of thunder and Dan asked his mother what it was.

"Tieng set danh," she answered, offering the Vietnamese word for thunder.

"No, American," Dan said.

He wanted to know the word for thunder in English. That showed how badly he wanted to learn English. He picked up his new language with the speed unique to children. He went into fourth grade, and never looked back. Years later, he would earn bachelor's degrees in electrical engineering and civil engineering.

Every new baby should be so lucky to have a loving mother like Kim, shown here with Christine.

***

In 1974, we were reassigned from Fort Gordon to Fort Huachuca, Ariz., where I would work in project management for the Communications System Agency. It would be my first and only active duty assignment where my daily uniform was Class A or dress greens. For all of my other assignments, I always wore the field uniform: fatigues.

Two weeks after settling in at Fort Huachuca, our daughter Christine, was born. It was more than four years after we married that Christine arrived. We had tried so long for a baby, that for a while we thought that it might not happen. When I took Kim to the hospital, her labor was a struggle, and I became alarmed at how long it was taking. I overheard someone in the hallway, say, "We have a bleeder." That scared me, knowing Kim's life was hanging in the balance. Finally, a doctor came out and said mother and baby were fine, but that Kim had lost a lot of blood and would be held in ICU overnight.

"I'm so cold," she told me, shivering from under the blankets in her hospital bed. I got my first look at Christine that day too, and like all new fathers, thought that this little miracle was a beauty. Christine gave me a little cry. Never have parents been happier to have a new baby. We might have liked to have had more children, but after Kim nearly bled to death, two seemed like enough. After all that we had gone through, and the drama in the delivery room at Fort Huachuca, there seemed to be no reason to risk Kim's life again.

***

In 1975, communist North Vietnam launched a massive offensive, and swept the South Vietnamese army before it. We watched the rout on TV. It seemed surreal as Soviet-made tanks broke through the gates of the presidential palace in Saigon, and refugees climbed to the rooftop of the American Embassy to flee in helicopters. After such a terrible investment of U.S. blood and treasure in Vietnam, it seemed impossible that the South Vietnamese would crumble so fast. We were saddened, shocked and disgusted by the rout. The communist takeover meant that communication between Kim and her family in Vietnam would be difficult and slow for more than a decade.

The same year that Saigon fell, I left active duty, as the U.S. Army went through a reduction in force, its third since 1971. Being caught in a RIF hurt, because I had earned strong efficiency reports, and I had served twice as a company commander, a battalion executive officer, and had completed the signal officer career course since returning from Vietnam. My boss at Fort Huachuca, Col. Morris LeFever, wrote an impassioned letter on my behalf asking the Department of the Army to retain me on active duty. I knew that the letter was futile, but I appreciated the gesture. There was no time for self-pity, or anger. I would not be burning my uniforms like another officer I knew. Somehow, I would keep my military career going, while moving into the civilian world, and providing for my family.

Fort Huachuca, Arizona, 1975

The dire situation called for a burst of activity. I crafted a resume emphasizing my management skills as a project officer for high-tech, high-dollar programs and as a company commander in Vietnam and at Fort Gordon. My resume would contain no mention of the mine and demolition warfare course I had completed, my eight campaigns during the Vietnam War, or even the three awards of the Bronze Star Medal. Instead, the focus would be on the procurement programs for satellite systems and microwave systems that I had worked on. My job search would emphasize my time as training officer for the 18,000-strong 1st Signal Brigade in Vietnam, helping train the South Vietnamese to take over the communications system the United States had installed there. The resume would tout my time as a hands-on manager performing communications system planning, monitoring circuit activation, as well as systems restoral, alternate routing, outages and reporting. Nowhere would I mention my primary specialty as a combat signal unit commander.

Maybe the telephone company or a communications-electronics manufacturer would be interested. I sent out packages to Ma Bell, to the Department of Defense, and even the Central Intelligence Agency, thinking maybe I could find the switch that would send me onto a parallel career track in the civilian world. At the same time, I explored getting on with my college education. I would need about 18 months of full-time enrollment to complete my bachelor's. We mulled staying in Arizona, which had grown on us and where I was already enrolled in the University of Arizona. Finally, however, we decided that it would be smarter to move back to my home state of Florida where I had family. Besides, I missed the lush green of Florida and the water. In the few months of active duty I had remaining, I enrolled at the University of South Florida, and was also scored an interview with an Army Reserve unit in Tampa that needed a communications officer.

Although a job offer failed to materialize, I figured we could scratch out a living between the G.I. Bill, and my Army Reserve pay. The $12,000 separation pay that I had received, after the IRS deducted $3,000, would provide a cushion. In those days, it seemed Vietnam service counted for little, and nobody was saying, "thank you for your service."

It was a crisis, but we had a plan, and the difficult transition to civilian life would bond Kim and I even closer.

24 – College

Almost all of the credit hours that I had earned at night at Augusta College and the University of Arizona transferred to the University of South Florida. Counselors told me I could get the rest of what I needed for a degree in about 1½ years as a full-time student. At USF, I could have gone in almost any direction, and pondered majoring in management, or becoming a dentist. But finally, I decided to go for something that I thought would be challenging, fulfilling for me, and a service to the community.

Released from active duty in 1975 after nearly 10 years in uniform, we got reacquainted with activities we had been missing, such as this family reunion. Kim makes sure Christine has enough while we relax under a shade tree.

Signal OCS grads had gone on to be generals, business leaders, and some had even achieved a measure of fame or notoriety. Several examples come to mind. Among them radical activist lawyer William Kunstler, Hutton Gibson, a Jeopardy grand champion in the 1960s and the father of actor Mel Gibson, and Marty Katz, a Hollywood film maker. Richard Green, who served as an OCS tactical officer during the Vietnam War, tracked down those tidbits while investing thousands of hours tracking down Signal OCS candidates from World War II, the Korean War and the Vietnam War. All had gone their own separate ways. I would seek a career in journalism, perhaps remembering my time as an apprentice pressman at the Florida Times Union in Jacksonville nearly 10 years earlier. The editors, columnists and reporters I had met made an indelible impression on me.

I think my father, and Kim, too, were somewhat disappointed in that career choice, coming as such a drastic change from where I had been heading. But I had hit a wall with plans to spend 20 years in the Army, and with my efforts to continue on the communications-electronics path in the civilian sector. The college life would be a challenge for me, and for the rest of the family. Dan was enrolled in his third school in his third state in just two years. Kim managed the house on little money and without complaint. At USF, I didn't broadcast that I was a Vietnam vet, but if anyone asked me about it, I would give them an honest answer. Frankly, it didn't seem that anyone cared what I had done in the military, or in anything that I had accomplished.

The Vietnam War was so unpopular at USF in the early 1970s that the only way students could enroll in ROTC was to cross-enroll in the program at the University of Tampa. It wasn't until December 1976 that the first five ROTC cadets were commissioned on campus at USF. However, there had been growing sentiment to offer ROTC at USF for several years. A 1972 student referendum on offering voluntary ROTC passed by a two-to-one margin. But in 1973, the Faculty Senate recommended rejection of ROTC on campus. It wasn't until 1975, my first year at USF, that the Student Senate, the Faculty Senate, the Council of Deans, and the USF Academics Program Council aligned and voted approval of ROTC.

No, college campuses were not the most welcoming places for the military uniform in the 1960s and the 1970s, but I found I got on well with the student journalists. One evening, Kim and I went to a campus presentation on Vietnam by Irwin Silber, co-editor of The Guardian newspaper, a radical left-wing newspaper. Not that I knew at the time that The Guardian was out of the mainstream.

I don't remember what Silber had to say, but I do remember that an Iranian student stood up to make a statement.

"All tape recorders should be shut off," he said, and announced that there would be a demonstration on the Tampa campus "for the Palestinian people and against the Zionists." He also announced that the flamboyant Nguyen Cao Ky, former prime minister of South Vietnam who had fled to the United States, would be in Gainesville. When Ky got to Gainesville, he would be met by demonstrators.

A couple of weeks later there was a scuffle on the USF campus as staff members from the student newspaper, The Oracle, covered Iranian students who were distributing pro-Arab, anti-Israeli literature. One of the Iranians shoved an Oracle photographer as he tried to take pictures. Obviously, the demonstrators had little regard for the First Amendment. I sometimes wondered what those Iranian students were doing a few years later when the U.S. Embassy staff in Teheran was taken hostage.

Being a family man, I had little time for college activities outside the classroom. I only wanted to finish my degree and find a job. I always felt a little out of place, older than the long-haired, sandal-wearing students with their seemingly effortless cool, who were tuned into a place that I could not, and would not, follow. Yet, with their bent for the counterculture, I was the true nonconformist. I wasn't going to influenced by any of the crazy political views some of the professors might have. With time I grew more comfortable in the classroom, and it showed. One of the hip young Oracle reporters liked a polyester shirt with flowering hibiscus design that I would occasionally wear, hideous as it was.

"Hey man, you need to wear that shirt more often," he would tell me, encouraging me to adopt a more relaxed demeanor.

I felt like I was doing more than co-existing. I had been accepted. Some of the students were marvelously talented and could wax rhapsodic over something as mundane as a junk yard. In my heart I knew that I could write, even if it tended to be a plain and choppy. With a little encouragement, however, from journalism instructor George Meyer, I volunteered as a staff writer for the student

114

newspaper. George had introduced me to the Oracle editors as one of his most talented students.

My first beat was covering student government. That gave me experience writing on deadline and clips for a portfolio that I could take to job interviews. Later I served as news editor for The Oracle. With the G.I. Bill, my Army Reserve pay, and the stipend I was paid for working at The Oracle, we managed to pay our bills, even though money was tight. I can vouch for the fact that college students might experience an intellectual bounty, but usually had nothing in their wallets. We even had a brush with the college drug culture.

We went to a student party south of Busch Boulevard on 26th Street. As the host showed us around, she introduced us to the other students who filled the house. Rock music was blaring out into the street. We paused when we saw students sharing a bong and smoking marijuana." Let's get out of here," I whispered to Kim. "One of the neighbors is going to call the cops and complain about all the cars and the loud music, and I don't want to be here when they come." We quickly left. Later, we heard that police had come knocking on the door after neighbors complained. Luckily for the students at the party, the police left after the music was turned down. Nobody was arrested.

In March of 1977, I finished my Bachelor of Arts in Mass Communications, the degree that Arlo Carter had dared me to pursue all those years earlier and began the search for my first newsroom job.

25 - The Glades

Newsroom clutter in 1982, and a disco shirt, too. It was a long way from the Vietnam War. The boxy thing in front of me that looks like a microwave oven is a minidisc terminal, our first newsroom computers. The machine with its fixed keyboard almost gave me carpal tunnel.

I relate to the great 1946 movie, "The Best Years of Our Lives." Fred Derry, played by Dana Andrews, is one of three veterans who return home from World War II and who struggle to get on with their lives as civilians. He comes home as an Army captain and decorated war hero. But the ribbons on his chest don't help him find a decent job. Though he is capable of so much more, the only job he can find is as a soda jerk. Fred is the classic good guy who just needs a little help, and there seems to be no one willing to give him a hand up, much less say "thank you for your service." There are a lot of Fred Derrys in the world, who struggle for a stake in the American dream.

In 1977, we started life over, me as a small-town newspaper editor in tiny Clewiston, Fla., and Kim as a stay-at-home mom. I might have preferred to have started at a larger newspaper, but the competition was fierce, and grads had already gobbled up most of the jobs before I got my degree. Journalism schools were crammed with students hoping to become Bob Woodward and Carl Bernstein and uncover the next Watergate. Newspaper editors had their pick of bright, talented journalists in those days, with a flood of idealistic grads coming out of J school, willing to work for next to nothing. So when my batch of resumes was met with no-opening responses, I accepted the first job offer extended to me. I was happy to go to work for Sonny Stalls, editor and publisher of the Clewiston News, located on the south shore of Lake Okeechobee, midway between Fort Myers and West Palm Beach.

"Most of the reporters we get here are either on the way up, or on their way down," Sonny told me.

I started work at Clewiston for $165 a week — not much money even in 1977. But slowly things got better. My first job was as editor of the Glades County Democrat, a weekly newspaper. It was a fine

Clewiston promo button: America's sweetest town.

title, but I did all the writing, photography and layout. The only other staff member was an elderly receptionist who was known to take out her dentures, place them on her desk, and take a nap at noon. I took many of my cues from Sonny Stalls, observing the way that he wrote stories, the conversational tone of his columns, which were often a humorous take on life in the Glades, the way he pasted-up the newspaper, and perhaps most importantly, the friendly, respectful, sometimes playful way he dealt with readers and local officials.

Sonny believed in pointing out local government folly, but not necessarily in continually berating officials, once he had made his point. Clewiston could be a little Peyton Place, like every other city and town. Sonny was in his early 50s at the time and was jogging for his health. He would smile and shake his head, marveling at the cars he spotted parked in the wrong driveways while he was jogging early in the morning. Sonny grew up in neighboring Moore

Haven, which he affectionately called "More Heaven." He had started work at the paper as a student, sweeping up the press room, eventually learning to run the press, cover local news, and then moving into the editor and publisher's chair. He knew the community. And through trial and error, Stalls found what worked in Clewiston.

"There is the right way to do things, the wrong way and the Sonny way," Stalls would say.

I worked hard to be accurate, and to show appropriate respect to readers and those I covered. I could tell that Sonny thought I had potential, and that he appreciated all the ground that I covered. Kim stayed in the Tampa area with the children until the school year ended. Meanwhile, I rented a room in Clewiston, and began looking for a house to buy. There was something unusual about Clewiston in those days. There was only one black person living in the city limits, and that was Al Graves, manager of the local Sears store. All the other black people lived in unincorporated Harlem, literally on the other side of the railroad tracks. The schools were integrated in Hendry County, as was the workforce, and soon enough the all-white and Latino nature of Clewiston neighborhoods began to change, too.

One night my landlady went off on a racial rant against Asian people. I'm not sure what provoked it, but I just held my tongue. Within a few months, school had ended in Tampa and we moved into the first house we had ever owned. I brought Kim by to introduce her to my landlady.

"I am sorry," the old woman said. "I didn't know your wife was Asian."

Kim and our son, Dan, were a minority of two in Clewiston. The only two Vietnamese people in town. Make that three if you include our half -Vietnamese daughter. I was concerned about them, but my concerns proved overblown. With Kim's industriousness, friendliness, and good heart, she soon made friends in the neighborhood. A bigger problem was stocking up on cooking supplies. To find a bottle of fish sauce, or a package of rice paper, we needed to drive an hour to either Fort Myers or West Palm Beach. And like families everywhere, we worked and

118

struggled to take care of the kids, and to put food on the table. Kim never changed from the young woman I met in Vietnam. She poured her life into the family and the children's needs, and remained the most selfless, loving person I ever knew.

"The children are number-one," she would tell me. "You're number-two."

Maybe we were isolated, but we were happy, and welcoming of the challenge. Other couples who had their lives turned upside down by the the Army's downsizing were not always so lucky. Some of our best friends from First Gordon divorced a few years afterward. I felt especially sorry for the husband who had been a military police captain, and whose brother had been killed in action in Vietnam. He lost his wife, a brother, and a career all within a matter of a few years.

At home in Clewiston: Dan, Kim and Christine.

***

As a small-town newspaper editor, our staple coverage was county commission, town hall, schools, crime, high school sports and the social scene, everything from marriages to births and deaths.

In the late 1970s, the drug wars were in full swing, and smugglers were flying planes into southern Florida, some of them crashing in the Glades. Several times I went to crash sites, and saw shattered aircraft and bodies, and everything from Quaaludes to bales of marijuana strewn on the ground.

Not to say that covering local government couldn't be exciting, too. I was covering a Moore Haven City Council meeting one night when the city's building official took offense at what a citizen said and knocked him to the floor. The official, a big, burly man moved toward the citizen, who was kicking at him from the floor. Instead of restoring order, the mayor and council just sat there. I jumped out of my seat, called the official's name, and put my arms around him.

"That's enough," I said.

He relaxed and sat down. They don't teach that in journalism school.

***

Fortunately, working at a newspaper also gave me license to watch people in a unique way, to come to know that everyone has a story, and that everyone has the potential to surprise. It also gave me a chance to watch a country changing fast. In the late 1970s, smoking in public was acceptable, but the mention of sex in a family newspaper was not. In the 1970s, we would never use the word "condom" in print, nor would we report on something called "safe sex." Yet that was to change. AIDS was coming to America, including the little towns in the Glades.

A couple of years after I went to work in Clewiston, the company was sold to a new owner and Sonny Stalls was let go. Soon after, Bernice Christiansen, the company bookkeeper, a woman with a sprightly sense of humor, a complete understanding of the books, and who was totally dedicated to the Clewiston News, was let go, too. I found myself without a valuable mentor.

Fortunately, there was Beryl Bowden. Beryl was retired as publisher and editor of the Clewiston News. She had given Sonny his start in the business. Beryl was a frequent visitor to the newsroom, where she would gently suggest story ideas and offer

120

critiques of the paper. She corrected my spelling of the word "privilege." It contains no "d," she said.

Or she might say, "The paper was a little thin this week."

When I needed a sounding board, I would drive to Beryl's house and sit in her quiet living room. We would talk town politics and she would tell me who were the good guys, and who were the bad guys. She would commiserate on the killing workload, and then I would go back to work feeling better. She was a true pioneer in Florida's glades area south of Lake Okeechobee, and put out newspapers for 27 years whether it was sunny outside, or a hurricane was blowing. Beryl was the publisher in the days when women might be relegated to writing a society column. There was a lot about Beryl that was atypical. She was a college graduate who had the courage to divorce her husband when things weren't working out. She had a double mastectomy in her 60s and beat cancer during a time when those odds were very long. She helped found the Clewiston Library, the Calusa Valley Historical Society, the Clewiston Museum, and a senior citizens club. She also carried on a lifelong correspondence and friendship with former Royal Air Force cadets from the United Kingdom who got their flight training near Clewiston during World War II.

We corrected a grievous omission by naming her editor emeritus of the Clewiston News, and later successfully nominated her for the Florida Press Association Hall of Fame. At that time, she was only the second woman to be inducted. Beryl Bowden wasn't a bad role model to be exposed to early in a career. She died at age 97 in 1998.

***

Kim made an appearance in the Clewiston News on July 25, 1979, when our features editor invited her to part in something called "Her favorite recipe." Kim shared her recipe for Vietnamese spring rolls. All the ingredients — ground lean pork, crab meat or shrimp, carrots and onions, an egg and salt — could be found in Clewiston. All the ingredients except 11-inch rice paper. For rice paper, we had to drive to the nearest specialty shop carrying Asian foods, meaning Fort Myers or West Palm Beach.

By this time, Kim had been driving about seven years, had gone back to high school to get her GED, and had taken up several hobbies including crocheting, gardening and fishing. She also went back to work. It was brave of her the way she went out on her own and put in applications. In her own words, here is how she describes entering the American workforce for the first time:

"I decided to go to work when Christine started kindergarten. I applied at the local Winn Dixie supermarket, left my application, then applied at Burger Queen. They hired me right away and had me making salads in the back. Shortly after that I was shopping in Winn Dixie and the manager asked me if I still wanted a job. I told him I already had a job. He asked me where, and how much I was making. I said $3.15 an hour."

"Come work with me and I will pay you $3.25 an hour," he said.

"I didn't think twice. I gave Burger Queen my two-week notice. They were so unhappy I was leaving but they didn't offer to raise my pay either. For my first six months at Winn Dixie, I worked as a cashier. Then they began training me in the other departments. First as a stocker, and then in the deli, and produce, and finally in general merchandise. Then they promoted me to general merchandise manager."

It was all new to Kim, but the manager quickly saw her potential.

"I didn't know anything about canned food. But I learned every day. I worked hard.

"I knew you had to treat the customers right. I didn't need to learn the work ethic. I already had that."

Others noticed her, too, and several other employers in Clewiston tried to lure her away.

"One of the bank managers came and asked me to go to work for his bank. I went and looked around the bank and decided that wasn't for me.

"I stayed at the Clewison Winn Dixie until 1985 when my husband was hired by a newspaper in New Smyrna Beach. The supermarket manager asked me not to leave, promising that if I stayed he would promote me to 'third man' — third in charge of the store.

"I told him that I couldn't. He gave me a good recommendation when I moved to my new home. I used that to get a job as general merchandise manager in my new town. I wasn't surprised at how well I did. I knew I could do it. I know myself. Work hard, be honest, give good customer service. That's important. I felt good about helping the family bring home the bacon. If not the bacon, at least a few little beans."

Somehow, a small-town newspaper editor, and a grocery manager were living the American dream, working hard, raising two kids, and owning our first home. In a small town, the newspaper editor can be something of a local celebrity, whether he wants to be or not. I found I could not go anywhere without being stopped by a reader with a complaint or compliment. Or having an angler who had just caught a big bass on Lake Okeechobee show up at my front door at night, wanting me to take a photo.

One time I was in Kim's store when someone walked up to me and said, "I know who you are."

Thinking, here we go again, I braced for the coming comment about the newspaper.

"You are Kim's husband," she said.

You are exactly right, I said, and left it there.

***

Kim had so little contact with other Vietnamese people and was speaking so much English all the time that she was getting a rusty in speaking her native language. But some of that isolation began to lift in 1985, when I took that new job in New Smyrna Beach.

26 - Ghosts of Vietnam

In 1985, as we were preparing to move to New Smyrna Beach where I would take a new job as editor of the News & Observer, we paused to attend the reunion of the Saint Augustine High School Class of 1965. It had been 20 years since my class graduated. It was the first time I would be able to attend a reunion. Refighting the Vietnam War was the last thing on my mind at the reunion. I should have known better. Somehow it seemed that the Vietnam War refused to remain in the past. The reunion had barely started when a classmate walked up and asked indignantly if I was ashamed of what I had done in the Vietnam War.

Kim and I in 1985, 20 years after the end of the Vietnam War.

Kim was standing right next to me. She had no idea what my classmate was talking about, and neither did I. But it wasn't difficult to figure out where he was coming from.

"Man, can't you give it a break?" I thought to myself.

It was 1985, 10 years after Saigon had fallen, and a dozen years since American troops had been withdrawn from Vietnam. It was 14 years since Kim and I had left Saigon. All I wanted to do was catch up on what my classmates had been doing. I was caught off-guard by the question.

"No," I replied to my classmate, holding my temper in check. "I am proud of my service."

I know that others returning from the Vietnam War were spit upon, called names, ostracized, I wasn't. But neither was I prepared for this venom coming so long after the war ended. Kim and I quietly walked away from my accuser and went to visit with other classmates. If there were any other reference to the war at the reunion, it was more typically, "We thought you died in Vietnam." Later, I found out that several of my classmates had served in Vietnam as well.

I can't say that I had a bad homecoming from the war, considering that I continued to serve on active duty for four more years before returning to civilian life. But given the climate in the country, I didn't talk about my experiences in Vietnam either, unless someone asked me about them. If anything, what I remember most was indifference. That was better than name-calling, or being accused of doing something immoral because I wore an Army uniform during wartime.

***

About the same time as that 20th high school reunion that I began to wonder about my old fishing buddy and best friend from high school. He had gone to Canada during the Vietnam War, and I had not seen him in 20 years. On a visit to Saint Augustine I drove to the house where my friend had grown up, and his mother gave me his address in south Florida. I sent him a Christmas card that year, and a few days later I received one in return. We talked once or twice on the phone and I learned that he had a new wife and two little boys.

In 1988, Kim and I were planning to visit our old friends from Vietnam, Fred and Hanh Freund, who also lived in south Florida, and thought maybe we could arrange a face-to-face meeting with my high school friend. I telephoned his house and got a busy signal. That meant he was home, I thought. I decided to drive over, all the while fighting down the feeling that perhaps I didn't know him anymore. Maybe we should just remain Christmas card acquaintances. I found his house and knocked on the door. His wife, who I had never met, came to the door.

"You are Jimmy Jones," she said.

She recognized me from a picture that she had seen. "Unfortunately, a lot of people tell me that I look just like my picture," I said.

She invited me in but said that her husband was fishing. "Come back at one o'clock, he will be thrilled to see you," she said.

A few hours later, I called his house and my friend answered the phone.

"Why didn't you tell me you were going fishing?" I asked, needling him like friends will do.

He hesitated. "I didn't know you were coming," he replied. I asked if it would be OK to drive over for a visit.

"Sure, come on over," he said quietly.

I began to wonder again whether this visit was a good idea. That feeling of unease vanished after our first handshake in 23 years. He looked a lot like he did in high school: trim, fit, but with gray in his hair, and he was wearing glasses.

"How come you don't have any gray?" he asked.

"Oh, but I do," I said, pointing to my temples, and my receding hairline.

"You look about like you did in high school," he said.

I kidded my friend about his middle name, and he responded that he remembered that my middle name was Alfred. There was a lot of catching up to do. We talked about an old classmate who wore
126

a flattop in high school who was now tending bar in Key West and wearing his gray hair down to his shoulders. My friend wanted to know how I ended upon the newspaper business. He had me pegged as an outdoorsman.

"I am not quite sure how it happened," I said. "I wanted to become either a newspaper man, or a dentist, but thought dentistry was too boring," I said, making a little joke.

My friend had done all right after the war. He owned a wall covering business. Down at his warehouse, he had a catamaran hanging from the ceiling. He had won a national championship racing sailboats a few years earlier. Unlike me, he continued to be an avid fisherman. Our two-hour meeting passed quickly, and there were a lot of things we didn't get around to talking about, including why he decided to go to Canada during the war and whether had any regrets. Not that I cared about that anymore. I saw no need to bring it up.

I drew my friend a map of how to find our house in New Smyrna Beach. If he dropped by some weekend, I planned to take him to the jetties at Ponce Inlet to try the fishing there. It never happened, and again we went our separate ways.

Time, distance, and history proved that we could never go home again.

27 – New Smyrna Beach

After working at weekly newspapers in the Clewiston-Belle Glade area for more than eight years, we moved to New Smyrna Beach in 1985, where I became managing editor of the News & Observer. The newspaper was published three days a week, and the owner, Peter Cardiff, was preparing to take it daily. Cardiff looked to me to lead the newsroom in the conversion to a six-day-a-week publication schedule in just a few months.

Our computers at the New Smyrna Beach News & Observer were cutting edge, and trouble prone.

Despite some trepidation by all of us in the newsroom, we made the change smoothly. Not to say that it wasn't a lot of work. You start every day with blank newsprint and have to fill it with something. There is never time to sit back and rest on your laurels. The readers and the owners want to know one thing: what have you done for me today? Added to that, perhaps aided by the stress, my jaw swelled ominously the weekend before the change to daily. Something like that always seems to happen on a weekend or a holiday.

That week I was in a dentist's chair getting a root canal. They are practically painless now, but back then they could be excruciatingly painful. As my orthodontist worked on me, lancing an abscess, he talked about a Lewis Grizzard column that the News & Observer had recently published. Grizzard was a humor columnist. It was clear my orthodontist found nothing funny in Grizzard's column and its treatment of dentists. He was really worked up about it. I was in agony, and all I could do was hang on. Never have I been so happy to get out of a chair.

***

New Smyrna Beach reminded me of St. Augustine, where I had grown up. It was on a river, and also the beach, and shared some of the same history as St. Augustine. Founded in 1768, by Dr. Andrew Turnbull, it was one of the largest English settlements in the New World, although most of the settlers were from the Mediterranean island of Minorca, and others were from Italy and Greece. New Smyrna was named after the birthplace of Turnbull's wife: Smyrna in Asia Minor. Today, Smyrna is known as Izmir, in Turkey. In colonial days, New Smyrna was a hot, jungle-like place with swarms of mosquitoes and the constant threat of Indian attack. After a relatively short time, many of the settlers revolted against the slave-like conditions and walked north to St. Augustine. The nation's oldest city, St. Augustine, founded in 1565, is proud of its residents who are descended from Minorcans. But New Smyrna had them first. Maybe I don't want to say too much about New Smyrna Beach, because I fell in love with the place. It had miles of wide, hard-packed beaches, as well as undeveloped Canaveral National Seashore, and thick primal forests. It had historic mysteries. Just what was Old Fort Park? And what was Sugar Mill Ruins? A sugar mill or a Spanish mission?

***

I had not lived in the same house with my mother since I was nine years old. Shortly after we moved to New Smyrna Beach, my mother and her fourth husband, Harry, came to visit and decided they liked the town. Soon they sold their home on the St. Johns River and moved a few miles away from where we lived. It had been almost a half century since I had so much contact with my mother. It would be pretty special. I enjoyed my mother's hug and kisses, her fried shrimp, and her mixed drinks. We often visited in each other's houses, and I saw more of my sisters, Phyllis and Sandi, who would come to visit. It caused a few complications, too. My stepfather, Harry, decided after a few years that he would run for mayor of neighboring Edgewater. Obviously, we couldn't endorse in that race because of the conflict of interest. Fortunately, he lost. Afterward, I told him he had a more important mission in taking care of my mom.

One time a couple of Hooters girls showed up in the newsroom in their short shorts and tight blouses, and announced I was "under arrest" for a local jail-and-bail charity. They hauled me down to a local restaurant in a two-seater sports car with one of the Hooters' girls in my lap. The things you have to do in the name of journalism! She apologized for the inconvenience. When we walked into the restaurant, I saw Harry and my mom having breakfast. They were startled. I explained the situation, and then began working the phones to raise my bail. When those Hooters girls showed up in the newsroom, it caused a bit of a stir at the front desk.

But it wasn't the only time. On another occasion, a brassy blonde was loudly causing a ruckus at the front desk.

"Where is that damned Jim Jones? He got me pregnant with these two kids and I haven't seen him since!" she said.

I walked out to see who the troublemaker was and there stood my sister Sandi, with her little boys, Mark and Kurt, visiting from Acworth, Ga. She had a big grin on her face. Just kidding, she said.

***

Probably for the first time in my newspaper career, I came to believe that I had my finger on the pulse of the community in New Smyrna, and for a third time, had a great woman as a mentor. The first had been Beryl Bowden in Clewiston, the former editor and publisher of the Clewiston News. The second was Beverly Hoot, who would become the commander of my Army Reserve unit in Tampa. And the third was Fran Hofreiter McGrath, the former editor of the News & Observer in New Smyrna Beach. Each of these great women took an interest in me and gave me invaluable encouragement.

Staying on top of the news is no easy thing, especially in a competitive environment. In Clewiston, the competition had been from the Fort Myers News-Press and the Palm Beach Post. In New Smyrna Beach, it was the Daytona News-Journal, which did not take kindly to having an upstart daily competitor just 16 miles away. The News-Journal stepped up its coverage and hired away three staff members. That hurt because we had a small staff to start with, and to have three leave at once without notice was challenging. But we didn't miss an issue. After a few tough weeks, we found replacements who would be with us for the long haul. Ironically, years later my family and I were in a pet store and ran into one of those who had jumped ship.

"You were the best boss I ever had," she said.

That made me feel a little better. As did one of the reporters who had deserted The Observer. He eventually asked me for a reference. I gave him a good one. As John Lennon once punned, "Time wounds all heels."

I discovered that being plugged into the community paid dividends in understanding the currents in New Smyrna Beach-Edgewater. I served on many boards, including the Chamber of Commerce, United Way, and Friends of Canaveral, which I co-founded. Friends of Canaveral came about after I had taken Christine fishing on the Mosquito Lagoon and noticed a ghostly house on the shore. The house was empty, abandoned, and decaying. I thought it would be a shame to lose that stately house, and wrote an editorial to stir up interest in its preservation. The superintendent of Canaveral National Seashore called and said he would work with me if I would round up local citizens interested in historic preservation to support the effort. Friends of Canaveral was successful, even though it took a decade to save the Eldora State House at Canaveral National Seashore. The house has been restored and now serves as an interpretive center on the Mosquito Lagoon.

In 1996, the year I turned 50, I was president of the Chamber, which at that time had about 600 members. The newspaper business was doing just what I had envisioned: keeping me at the

131

heartbeat of the community, serving as a watchdog on local government, and providing an important service to readers.

In 1998, the Southeast Museum of Photography in Daytona Beach hosted "Vietnam Legacy," which showcased the book "Requiem," a collection of pictures taken by photographers who had lost their lives in Vietnam. Often times the images were taken from film still in their cameras when they died. Vietnam Legacy also included a companion collection, "Tet Plus 30: Central Florida Remembers Vietnam." The photos were by local Vietnam vets, including me. I was a reluctant participant because my photos are so personal. During the war, I deliberately chose not to photograph dead bodies, Viet Cong prisoners, or even have someone snap a photo of me in my steel pot and flak jacket, hefting an M-16. I didn't want to alarm my family, and besides I had not served in the boonies. I had been a Signal Corps officer.

Nevertheless, the museum borrowed 11 of my photos.

One day I was standing in the museum with Tim Page, who had curated the book with Horst Faas. Page noticed a date on the display incorrectly said that the war ended in 1976. The war actually ended in 1975. Page asked for the mistake to be corrected, saying that the North "liberated" the South in 1975.

"I beg your pardon," I said. "The South wasn't liberated, it was conquered."

Page, an Englishman who was wounded several times while covering the Vietnam War, said that Americans are still too hung up on the war and refuse to accept what happened there. Again, I disagreed, and said the "liberation" he spoke of didn't occur while I was in Vietnam, nor did it happen during the time that millions of Americans served there. Just ask the hundreds of thousands of Vietnamese boat people who fled the conquering communists, and ask how liberated they felt. I couldn't resist adding that in the war of ideas, the idea of a free market seemed to be winning out in the communist nation. Page replied that the Vietnamese always pick and choose what they want from their foreign influences.

I agreed. We left it there.

132

28 — A last hurrah

James A. Jones Sr., with grandchildren Stacey, left, and Christine.

My father was having one of the happiest and most successful retirements of anyone I ever knew. Luckily, I was back in his neighborhood after being so far away for so many years. I could share in the fun. I was just an hour away in New Smyrna Beach, making it easy to drive to Saint Augustine for a visit. After he retired from the City of Saint Augustine, he began buying MGBs, — a fixed roof version of the little British MG sports car — as a hobby. He often had as many as three MGBs parked under the pines in the yard at one time that he would tinker with when he felt like it. He usually had one that ran. He found relaxation in piddling in his home garden, where he grew all kinds of things: eggplant, okra, squash, corn, watermelons, cucumbers, onions, peanuts, and more. My dad even planted lemon grass, one of Kim's favorite cooking ingredients, as we moved about in the Army, and later in civilian life. He did it because Kim used lemon grass so much in cooking, and she was afraid she would lose her source with all the moving. But of all the things he grew, it was datil

My dad's mother, Sallie Blache Jones, came to visit him in Saint Augustine in the early 1950s. He is wearing his World War II Ike jacket.

peppers which most challenged and intrigued him. Datils are to Saint Augustine, what onions are to Vidalia, Ga. They combine heat and a flavor like no other.

He began turning datils into sauce, constantly experimenting with his recipe until he perfected it.

"He always put so much love, time and money into making the sauce, from growing and caring for the plants, and saving bottles," my sister Phyllis remembers.

"Not to mention what the heat from those peppers did to his hands when he cut them and removed the seeds. The heat would burn him right through gloves," she said.

Finally, Phyllis bought him labels for his bottles reading "Jimmy Jones Hot Sauce, The Best Little Hot Sauce in Florida." That was the final push he needed to sell his hot sauce to stores and bars around St. Augustine.

"I just felt like his hot sauce should have a name," Phyllis said. "So, I thought of a name for the sauce and went to the man who did the printing for our business and put the order in. He loved the label."

He also became active in Veterans of Foreign Wars, and in the VFW's Cooties organization, that visited veterans' hospitals to cheer up patients. He loved travel, whether it was driving to Arizona, New Mexico, or Virginia to visit family. He embraced the CB radio craze and jawboned with others on the long drives using the handle "Green Hornet." If he saw a driver in distress on the side of the road, he would stop and try to help them get their car running. At no charge. One of his favorite family activities was gathering oysters from the sloughs around Saint Augustine and roasting them in the back yard over an open fire. It didn't matter that he was allergic to most seafood and couldn't eat the oysters. He presided over those oyster roasts shirtless and barefoot, wearing a pair of old shorts, and sipping from a can of beer.

In the company of his children and grandchildren, and a little mutt of a dog named "Lady," that's when he was the happiest. But shortly we moved to New Smyrna Beach in 1985, my father got a dreaded diagnosis. He had Lou Gehrig's Disease, amyotrophic lateral sclerosis. The incurable progressive neurodegenerative disease was causing his muscles to waste away. He once had forearms like Popeye's. Now became a shadow of his former self. He needed his two arms to scratch his face, one arm lifting the other. It was startling and heartbreaking to see how fast his physical condition deteriorated. When he fell ill, I knew there was a rapidly closing window of opportunity to sit him down and interview him on video to capture his memories of family history.

He told me that he could not wait to get off the farm during the Great Depression. He quit farming one season after making just enough money to buy a new set of work clothes for the next crop. There are a lot of details in those interviews that would have otherwise been lost to memory. Years later, I was able to put those interviews on DVDs and share them with other family members. My sister Sandi had her two grown sons, who were born after his death, watch the DVDs with her to get a sense of the man their grandfather had been.

In his last couple of years of life, he was able to give away my sisters Sandi and Kathy in marriage, and then less than a year before he died, saw me promoted to lieutenant colonel in Orlando. Or more accurately, I should say that he got to see me as the promotion ceremony was breaking up. My little brother Tony was bringing him to the ceremony from Saint Augustine and got him there a little late.

Kim pins on the silver oak leaf, marking my promotion to lieutenant colonel.

"You mean we drove all this way to be late?" Tony said.

Even so, it was such a proud and happy day for our family. Kim pinned the silver oak leaf of a lieutenant colonel on my collar, with the help of the commanding general. I was happy that my father lived to see me receive this final promotion. He knew that I had pulled myself up by my bootstraps, and had earned my promotion the hard way — much as he had fought and struggled in his own life.

Two days before his death in March of 1987, I drove up from New Smyrna Beach to Saint Augustine to see him with my little girl, Christine. My father always liked beer — whatever was on sale at the grocery was his favorite brand. So we had an Old Milwaukee together. We visited for several hours. I told him that I loved him. Christine gave him a hug and a kiss. A warm smile played across his face. I'll never forget that look. My dad knew death was near and said he was looking forward to seeing his late mother again. As he lay in the bed, he said he had seen her face in the wall. He had extraordinary love for her.

We got word two days later that he had passed away, and Kim and I drove to Saint Augustine that night. When we arrived at his home in Saint Augustine, a half can of beer — the one he had with me — was still in the refrigerator. At his funeral service, relatives, some of whom had been feuding for years, put aside their differences and drove down from North Carolina and Virginia to pay their respects.

Charles Butler, one of my cousins who rose from humble beginnings to a successful career with French's mustard company, recalled that when he was 16 he came to my dad with his 1941 Ford that had lost its brakes. My dad took the time to help, and Charles never forgot it. Twelve years after my father's passing Charles mentioned the incident to me at a family reunion. Those warm thoughts, expressed so many years later, meant much to me. That same year, I left the active Reserve, after 21½ years of active and reserve duty.

As I processed out as a drilling reservist, I mentioned to someone that I might get back into uniform someday.

"I doubt it, I've never seen anyone do it yet," he said.

He proved to be right. I was proud of my service, but it was time to focus even more on journalism and my family.

Kim stands on a beach walkway in New Smyrna Beach, after 25 years of marriage.

29 – Cake

Kim finally got her wedding cake in 1995, 25 years after we were married in Long Binh, Vietnam. We lost the first cake in 1970, when the Saigon police hauled everyone and the car down to police headquarters. I was left at the altar waiting for hours wondering what had happened to the bride, thinking maybe Kim had skipped out on me. We had been a victim of circumstances beyond our control. We rescheduled the wedding for a couple of days later. This time, I wouldn't leave it to anyone else to get Kim to Long Binh Chapel. I drove an Army Jeep to Saigon and brought Kim to Long Binh for the wedding. But there had been no time or energy to order a new cake.

That is until 1995, when my mother threw an anniversary party for us at the Islander, a resort located on beachfront at New Smyrna. We invited friends that we had known over the past 25 years and told everyone -- except Kim. All we told Kim was that we would celebrate the anniversary with the kids, Dan and Christine, over dinner at the Islander. She was grumpy as we walked into the Islander, because she didn't understand our odd behavior. We had given her no say in where we were going. Then she began seeing old friends, one after another. It seemed to her like a ridiculous series of coincidences. Until she bumped into Chin Klein, an old friend from her hometown of Bac Lieu with whom she had worked at Soc Trang Army Airfield. Kim and Chin squealed with delight as they embraced. Chin had flown into town from California. Finally, the ruse was up.

It had been impossible for friends and relatives to attend the wedding, but now here they were at the Islander to help us celebrate an unforgettable anniversary. My beautiful Kim had wedding cake, dancing, the company of good friends, and champagne, too.

Old friends celebrate a surprise 25th wedding anniversary.

30 - Encounters

At the risk of getting off the path of this love story and life struggle, I think it's worth noting some of the highlights of my life in newspapers. This crazy newspaper career hasn't been all controversy, confrontation and hard work. It's also been fun too, bringing me in contact with famous people, some folks who were great characters, and some who were just great.

John Glenn gives a good, old-fashioned scolding to the media.

In 1998, I had the opportunity to be scolded by John Glenn, the first American to orbit the Earth. Actually, there were about 100 of us, reporters and photographers, who received the scolding. We had gathered at Kennedy Space Center's launch pad 39B for a question-and-answer session with Glenn and his six crew mates on the shuttle Discovery. Glenn was a robust 77, and he seemed to glow, to stand out from the mere mortals who comprised the rest of the crew. His return to space that year would be his first since 1963, a span of 36 years.

"Let me castigate the press a moment here," Glenn said." Too often you get into the human aspects of this and you don't get into the scientific stuff that gets into everybody's houses all over the country. It's easy to report the 'oh, gee whiz 'of launches", Glenn said, urging journalists to dig deeper. If Americans understood the benefits of science derived from the space program, there would not be the chronic funding problem, he said. Glenn's scolding was so direct and honest that no one seemed to mind. In fact, the scolding was an honor.

There were others, too, who never achieved or aspired for national renown but who got under my skin, and into my heart. Buddy

Richardson was one of them. As a 26-year-old Marine during the Korean War, he had been stabbed with an enemy bayonet in hand-to-hand combat, suffered a broken jaw and lost an eye, as well as the feeling in some of his fingers and toes. In 1990, Buddy, then 65 years old, was still fighting for his comrades, the veterans. One day he pulled up to the newspaper in his battered red pickup and dragged me outside.

"Come out here I want you to see something," Buddy said.

His passenger was a fellow vet, with a leg that had been amputated just blow the hip. Buddy was taking the man to the veteran's hospital in Gainesville in his truck and was angry that the government wasn't doing more to help the man. Buddy hauled lots of vets to the hospital or veteran's clinic, vets who would otherwise have had no transportation. The long ride could be uncomfortable in Buddy's truck, which lacked air conditioning, especially for an amputee or someone in pain. The vet with one leg asked Buddy to get him a newspaper.

"Your money is no good here," Buddy said, digging in his pocket for change. I waved Buddy off, and handed him a paper. "No charge for him," I said, feeling very small at Buddy's example.

Buddy was constantly on the alert for slights against veterans, real or perceived, and there were plenty of them in the days before the First Gulf War and the terrorist attacks of 9/11, when America seemed to have turned its back on vets, especially those from the Korean and Vietnam wars.

"I'm the kind of person who doesn't want to see them stepped on or squashed," Buddy said. "I don't think our vets are properly taken care of or looked up to for what they went through."

Before he was finished, Buddy led a drive to put a monument in the local cemetery identifying veterans of all wars.

"I have had wives call me and ask that their husband's name be placed on the plaque and they cry. Sometimes I cry with them," Buddy said.

He also built a "choo-choo" train and caboose on the chassis of a couple of pickup trucks. He filled both with veterans 'memorabilia and drove the train in local parades. His home was a clutter of bedpans and wheelchairs for vets. He taught himself to type, all the better to help motivate unresponsive government officials. He was a short, balding man with thick glasses and a hearing aid in each ear. He was one of the most beautiful men I ever knew, and a true American hero.

Continuing into 2018, the United States continued to fail its veterans in providing the health care they were promised.

***

One of New Smyrna Beach's most fascinating and distinctive characters was Ken Smiley. At 6 foot 1, he had a full beard, and long blond hair worn in dreadlocks. He wore shorts, a light-colored shirt, and slip-on shoes. He walked everywhere or rode his green bike, and slept on the beach. He was a native of Waltham, Mass., but grew up in southern California, and was wounded in Vietnam. Ken was a familiar sight in town, known to waitresses, as well as the supervisor of elections. Over the years, he filed paperwork to run for governor and president of the United States on the "Commonest Party" ticket. Fire came into Ken's eyes when he talked about religion and wrongs he saw in the world.

"Our dominion on Earth is to make peace with the planet. Jesus says we are supposed to love everyone. We are not here to mutilate the place," he said.

He would eliminate meat from the diet. "These teeth are for greens and fruit. Not for eating meat," he said. If he were in charge, Ken said he would do something about automobiles and 50,000 traffic deaths a year, and the plague of alcoholism. He would clean up the environment and teach boys not to grow up to hit women. He suggested paying people by their age and using space in public buildings for homeless people. As for who should be in charge, he suggested selecting a high school student, or letting the gubernatorial candidates settle it with a stakes race down on the beach. Ken Smiley and I were 180 degrees apart on most everything, but when I saw his healthy glow and lack of stress, I thought wistfully, maybe this guy is onto something.

142

***

Mimi Henchy died of cancer March 4, 1998, at Halifax Medical Center. That is nearly 20 years ago, and yet her loss remains with Kim and me. She was our friend, and she died a painful death from an aggressive form of cancer. We also remember that she had no medical insurance, how we fought to get her relief from her pain, and to be admitted to a hospital. That should not have been the case then, nor today when the United States still has not figured out how to provide everyone with affordable healthcare. Mimi, a native of Vietnam, became seriously ill less than a year before her death. She went to a dentist with what she thought was a toothache. Her dentist referred her to a physician, who referred her to Moffit Cancer Center in Tampa. The diagnosis: terminal cancer.

Back home in Edgewater, she was in tremendous pain, unable to work, without health insurance or financial means, and uncertain about what to do next. Kim implored me to do something. On a Sunday, I called a volunteer with the American Cancer Society, who said Mimi should go to see a doctor on Monday, who could refer her to the oncology program at Bert Fish Medical Center in New Smyrna Beach. Monday morning, I began calling, reaching three doctors' offices and the administrator at the hospital. Dammit, somebody was going to do something. It wasn't right that someone have a life-threatening illness and not be in treatment. Not have their pain under control. Not in the United States of America. And not in my town that had a tax-supported hospital.

It wasn't long before I got call backs, with one of the doctors saying Mimi should go to the emergency room. Later that morning I found a telephone note on my desk from Mimi's boyfriend. Mimi was sitting alone in the waiting room at the hospital. I left work and went to the hospital, where I saw Mimi sitting alone, shivering. I sat down next to her and held her hand. Minutes later, a kindly Pink Lady volunteer came over, put her arm around Mimi, and took her back to see the doctor. Mimi was admitted and then transferred to the hospital in Daytona Beach, where they got her pain under control and started chemotherapy, and later radiation treatment. She was able to come home briefly, before being readmitted and passing away soon after.

The weekend after her death, family and friends gathered a Mimi's house. Her spirit seemed palpable in the screened room overlooking her backyard with its banana and papaya trees. It was her favorite place. A wind chime clinked delicately in the breeze, carrying the bewitching scent of blooming citrus. Inside the house, we saw the framed pictures of her children and the trophies that they had won. There was also a framed picture of Mimi, looking radiant in her wedding gown.

It was heart-wrenching watching her children quietly read her obituary. The older child, a daughter, was a college student studying computer technology. The youngest child was a little boy, very much into baseball card collecting. Mimi had always been so full of life. She loved to sprint through the shallows at the beach and enjoyed nothing more than visiting with friends around a table full of food. She was brave until the end. When she would see Kim and me, she would say "My good friends," and give us a hug,

People come and go but we will always remember Mimi.

Take care of yourself. Take care of your friends. Appreciate your friends and your life. Neither lasts forever.

31 - Jack Mitchell

Photographers often don't get photographed, so I asked Jack Mitchell to sit for me in his New Smyrna Beach studio. I shot this photo with my 35 mm film camera. Jack was happy with the image, and I was too.

An angry Jack Mitchell was on the line, calling me from New York City. I had long wanted to meet Jack. The noted photographer had grown up in New Smyrna Beach and gone on to a storied career in New York. And now I had offended him without knowing why. Talk about getting off on the wrong foot with someone. Although best known for his portraits of dancers and others from the arts world, his most famous images were of John Lennon and Yoko Ono after they completed their Double Fantasy album. The album marked a comeback for the couple after being away from the recording studio for five years.

In November 1980, the Lennons went into Jack's New York photo studio at East 74th Street for photos intended for the New York Times. It turned out to be the last time Lennon would ever venture into a photo studio. A photo from that session was used on People magazine's cover after Lennon was killed on Dec. 8, 1980, becoming its best-selling issue.

Jack demanded to know why we used his portrait of John and Yoko in our weekly entertainment section without crediting him as the photographer. I apologized to Jack for the omission and explained that the photo was included in a syndicated entertainment package we had purchased. We had simply neglected to include a photo credit.

Fortunately, I knew that Jack had learned his photo skills in New Smyrna Beach, studying Hollywood promotional photos of the stars of the 1930s and 1940s to learn the secrets of lighting, and practicing his portrait skills on family members, teachers and others before serving in the U.S. Army during World War II. After a little discussion, Jack simmered down, accepted my apology, and even offered to let The New Smyrna Beach Observer, his hometown newspaper, use images from his archive. As long as we supplied the mandatory photo credit.

I invited Jack to stop by the Observer's newsroom to meet the staff the next time he was in New Smyrna Beach, and to let me buy him lunch.

"I would like to do that," Jack said. I asked Jack how he knew about our photo credit screwup on the John and Yoko picture. "My sister called me," he said of Avis Shibley, who still lived in the New Smyrna Beach area at the time.

I got to know Jack and his life partner Bob Pavlik well. And I also got to know Avis, whose modest house was filled with Jack's portraits of the who's who of the arts and entertainment world. Jack loved Avis, who had been one of his subjects as a dark-haired teen beauty while he was learning the art of portrait photography. Jack made his reputation as a dance photographer, but also made portraits of many other cultural icons, including Tennessee Williams, Gloria Swanson, Meryl Streep, Jack Nicholson, Andy Warhol, Edward Albee, Salvador Dali, and many more. Avis had a sensational collection of her brother's portraits, perhaps the best and largest outside of any museum collection.

The next time Jack flew in from New York to visit his mother who lived on New Smyrna's Canal Street, he stopped by the newsroom, met the staff, and agreed to sit for an interview and photo. We put the story and photo on The Observer's front page to introduce him to folks who didn't know Jack and allow old friends to see what he had been up to. From that point on, we became friends and, in a sense, collaborators. Jack was generous and gracious, quick witted, a deep thinker, and a great conversationalist who could regale you for hours with stories about those he photographed. He was an artist who worked to capture something of the soul of his subjects in his exquisitely made portraits. He often did much of the printing himself in the darkroom to achieve the deepest blacks and all the other shades in between to white.

"I am not in the flattery mode. I like to make people look the way they are," he once told me.

Jack's sense of timing in his dance portraits reflected his knowledge of that art form, and the high trust and respect

147

that dancers had for him. The great Alvin Ailey sought Jack out to photograph his dance troupe. Years later, Jack turned the Ailey photos into a book. Even though Jack had not graduated from college, he was a voracious reader and his home library was stocked with the classics and books on the history of Greece and Italy. He loved classical music, and history. Our wide-ranging conversations would cover almost everything except sex — he was a committed gay man and I a confirmed heterosexual. Not to say that Jack didn't have a salty sense of humor.

I was fascinated with the fact that Jack had met and photographed John and Yoko and was curious about what that experience was like. Jack told me that John was warm and witty but seemed worn beyond his 40 years by the rock and roll life he had lived. Yoko was quieter, more reserved, and had a smile that disappeared as quickly as she flashed it. It was probably a relief for the Lennons that Jack was not a Beatlemaniac — his tastes ran more to opera, Broadway musicals, and Beethoven. This allowed the Lennons to relax and enjoy the late-night photo session. The Lennons came in wearing glasses, and after a few shots Jack asked that they be removed because of the glare. Seeing that I was a Beatle fan, Jack dropped a line that I'll never forget: "The next time I am down this way, I'll bring you a print." I think my heart skipped a beat. I would never have been so bold as to ask for anything from Jack, but I was excited by the promise of a first generation print from his negative.

True to his word, the next time Jack was in town he brought a rolled up 19-by-15-inch print and instructed me to have it framed using archival matting and UV glass. Jack was always very precise in ensuring that his prints were treated properly. The amazing black -and-white image hangs in my home today and will become a family heirloom. Years later, Jack allowed me to look through the guest book of signatures from his photo subjects, and among them was a John Lennon autograph with the classic doodle of John, Yoko, and Sean.

In 1993, my daughter Christine and I visited Jack in his New York studio. Opening the door and going inside the building, we saw a row of mailboxes, including one with an inconspicuous card labeled only with" J Mitchell." We pushed a button on the mailbox, and moments later we were buzzed inside. Jack was standing there to greet us, tall, thin, dressed all in black, with a friendly smile and an outstretched hand of welcome. Walking into Jack's studio was impressive, not because of its magnitude — because it was relatively

Kim and I joined Jack Mitchell at the Southeast Museum of Photography, Daytona Beach in April of 1996. Jack had gifted a number of his photographs to the museum.

modest in size — but because of the portraits that lined the walls, including Warren Beatty and Robin Williams, and all those dancers. One of the largest, however, was of piano virtuoso Vladimir Horowitz, the same photo used on Horowitz 'last album of music recorded in his lifetime.

Jack was good enough to show us around his darkroom and studio, where I turned the tables and took several photos of Jack using the same battered 35 mm Pentax that I had carried in Vietnam. Jack seemed a little uncomfortable as I

149

clicked off several shots. He latched onto an aluminum pole that held a spotlight with a red filter and offered a bit of coaching.

"It's always good to give your subject something to hold onto," Jack said. He showed us proofs of an upcoming book titled Alvin Ailey American Dance Theater: Jack Mitchell Photographs." It was a retrospective of the 32 years Jack had spent photographing the Ailey troupe.

"I did this book because I wanted to. The other books were done as career-building things to get myself better known. This book I consider historic. Not so much for me but because of who I photographed. I am very proud of this book," Jack said. Left unsaid was that Jack was a white son of the South photographing a brilliant, pioneering black dance company. It was not about race, it was about the art.

The many faces of Jack Mitchell reflected at the Flamingo Follies in New Smyrna Beach.

Afterward we walked to a nearby restaurant and dined on grilled tuna. Jack hailed a cab, and at his recommendation, Christine and I went to Mickey Mantle's restaurant for a bowl of rice pudding.

150

On several other occasions, I took Jack's photo in his studio because I knew that the photographer doesn't often get his photo taken. Jack then took my camera and shot a few photos of me. Looking at those photos now, I am not particularly pleased with the way I look, and never have been. But as Jack said, he was not in the flattery mode.

One time at a New Smyrna Beach art festival, I captured an image of Jack peering into a mirror sculpture and sent an enlargement to him. Jack liked the photo so much that he sent me a thank you note. He had impeccable manners and was very old-fashioned in that way,

"Thanks so much for the great color enlargement of the photo you took of my many faces at Flamingo Follies. It is a flattering image and I love it!" he wrote.

He was very generous in praising the work of others. On one occasion, he suggested a photo series on childhood, "Growing Up in Paradise," inspired perhaps by his own happy memories of growing up in New Smyrna Beach. The exhibition, photographed by Observer staff, was curated by Jack himself, and displayed in a local gallery. Before Jack retired from New York and moved back to New Smyrna Beach, he would often return home to visit his mother and other family members.

On one occasion I drove a pickup truck and met Jack and Bob at a New Smyrna Beach health club where they had been working out. They climbed into the bed of the truck and I drove them to The Breakers bar for hamburgers. I think that the great photographer enjoyed the ride, and my audacity in presuming to cart him around like that. Several years later, after Jack had moved to a two-story house on Live Oak Street in New Smyrna Beach, he prepared another book," Icons and Idols."

In reading Jack's narrative, I realized he was not only a great photographer, but a fine writer as well. I praised his skill as a storyteller as he shared his rise from a small Florida railroad town.

His sister Avis once told me Jack might have starved after he moved to New York without the food packages his family mailed to him from Florida. Eventually, Jack's career caught fire, as evidenced in Icons and Idols, and his finances improved. Jack shared with me the proofs of the upcoming book, one masterpiece of a portrait after another. I urged him to use one of the John and Yoko portraits on the cover, and he did. Jack planned his work so well that am sure that was his plan anyway. I wrote the first story announcing the arrival of Icons and Idols and shared the story with the Associated Press which meant that it was available to newspapers coast to coast. As long as I worked in New Smyrna Beach, Jack generously shared photos from his extensive archive when one of his subjects made news or passed away. It was a valuable gift from someone who had been a regular contributor to the New York Times.

The most fun that we had away from work and photography was sharing a meal at one of our homes. Bob Pavlik was a gourmet cook, as was my wife Kim. I'll never forget a mango pudding that Bob made for one dinner, or his delight in discovering ingredients Kim used in her cooking." Cilantro!" he once exclaimed after biting into one of her Vietnamese spring rolls, which I think are the best in the world. It was also fun to hear Jack dish on his latest encounters with luminaries.

"We went to the opening of The Ailey Company at City Center last night," Jack wrote from New York in 1993. "Denzel Washington, Dionne Warwick, Jessye Norman and Al Jarreau were there."

Another note from Jack: "Recently did a good happy shot of Jane Pauley of NBC which ran in the New York Times Sunday before last. She is a charmer."

Years later, I also had the opportunity to photograph and interview Pauley when she came to Sarasota. Jack was correct. Jane is a charmer, and makes you feel very much at ease when you talk to her. I even showed Jane some old photos from Vietnam of Kim and I and she seemed genuinely interested. Even though Jane Pauley and I are worlds apart, we are both baby boomers, shaped by so many events after World War II. Jack continued in that letter, which is interesting in what he says about his subjects and how he photographed them:

"Last week Linda Lavin (TV Alice) came to my studio along with make-up, hair/wig man, costumer, ad agency rep, personal p.r. man and two p.r. people from the show Gypsy. They, along with my assistant and two dressers filled my little studio. She is replacing Tyne Daly as the lead in the show next month and I was asked to take the color poster/ad photograph which will also go up HUGE outside the theater.

"She was really not into the role yet, but I got such an incredibly beautiful shot, many good ones, but one which defines the role of Mama Rose. I had done Tyne also. She was too fat to wear the white fox fur, but I had Linda wear it over her red dress. Shot it against a thunder gray seamless with a bright magenta light coloring the upper center of the background, then a gridded light just illuminating face and upper body (like a fuzzy spotlight), hit the white fur with a rim light of magenta on one side and put another gridded white light on bottom part of seamless to semi silhouette the lower body ... Everyone is pleased ... am thrilled but anxious to see exactly what the designer does."

After Jack's retirement, he moved back to New Smyrna Beach, and bought a home on Live Oak Street, where he continued to work, produce new books, photograph the artists in residence at Atlantic Center for the Arts, and showcase his art in shows around the country.

Even after Jack Mitchell retired, He never stopped working. He is shown above going through his archive of negatives in his home office in 1998.

Jack was particularly pleased that the DeLand Museum of Art put together a joint exhibition of photos by Yusuf Karsh and himself in 1997. Undoubtedly, Jack had studied Karsh's photo technique as be developed his own skills. He would also make himself available to the public and occasionally show slides of his work at the New Smyrna Beach Library, offering a running commentary, provoking laughter and chuckles from his rapt audience.

In 1999, dismayed by the lack of growth of the New Smyrna Beach Observer, and disappointed in its ownership and management, I accepted a new job on Florida's west coast at the Bradenton Herald. It was tough to move away, considering that my mother still lived in the New Smyrna Beach area, and I would be leaving behind so many good friends. Even so, I still stayed in touch with Jack long distance and would occasionally stop by for a short visit.

In 2005, Jack celebrated his 80th birthday with many close friends, the majority of which brought gifts of Tanqueray Gin, his favorite. He wrote Kim and I a thank you note, and in classic Jack style he wrote: "It was good to see you — and very special you would travel that distance. And thank you for supporting my drinking. Thank you for the best gin! Love to you both. Jack"

154

A few years prior to Jack's death Nov. 7, 2013, he had fallen on a swimming pool deck outside his home and broken his back. The injury left Jack, who had previously stood ramrod straight, hunched over, and made it difficult for him to work in the darkroom. Before Jack was fully recovered, his partner Bob, who had been beset by health problems, died. "I always thought I would go first," said Jack, the older of the two.

But that didn't keep him from assembling photos for another book, which hopefully someday will be published. I last saw Jack on his 88th birthday in September, two months before his death, when I stopped by with French pastries and well wishes. It didn't occur to me that he might be near death, even though he was more stooped and drawn than I had seen him before. Whenever I would call to check on him, he would say his vitals were near perfect. Like many others who knew Jack and were lucky to call him friend, his death was deeply felt. I knew him as a close friend, a gentleman, a rare human being, and something of a father figure. And yes, I loved him, and miss him.

The New York Times published an extensive obituary. The primary photo of Jack was credited to the Associated Press, but I knew that I had taken it in his New Smyrna Beach Beach studio in 1999. I still have the negative. How appropriate, I thought, that the Times would use my photo without my credit, considering how Jack and I had made our introductions so many years earlier.

32 - Unchained Melody

Ringo Starr brought his All Starr Band, including John Entwistle from The Who and Randy Bachmann from Bachmann Turner Overdrive to Orlando on Aug. 5, 1995. That's when I found out that among the many facets of Kim's personality, she is a little rock 'n' roller, too. Ringo quickly got the crowd on its feet with classics like "Yellow Submarine" and "It Don't Come Easy." Or should I say, Ringo had us all dancing and cheering on our chairs?

The great Bo Diddley with Gov. Lawton Chiles on Sept. 20, 1998.

Including Kim.

I knew she was a frustrated dancer — frustrated to have a tangle-footed mate like me — but I didn't know she could get into the music with such abandon! An unexpected bonus was meeting Beatle George Harrison's sister, Louise, backstage. She had driven over from Sarasota hoping for a meeting with Ringo to promote her We Care Global Family, which was trying to do what it could for our ailing planet. She signed a photo card for me, wishing me "love and laughter." Ringo's concert was fun and emotional, and went right to the heart of baby boomers that night. I had the opportunity in 1993 to meet Stephen Stills, the rocker who performed "For What It's Worth" with Buffalo Springfield, "Suite Judy Blue Eyes "with Crosby Stills and Nash, and "Love the One You're With" as a solo single. Stills was in the New Smyrna Beach area taking a turn as a guest disc jockey at a radio station owned by oilman Reid Hughes who was running for state office. Essentially, Still's appearance was a favor for Hughes, who was known as a staunch environmentalist.

Stephen Stills, 1993.

I was invited to the radio studio to meet Stills, and also to a reception that night when he played an acoustic guitar and sang to a crowd in a hotel lobby. Dressed in a Hawaiian shirt, jeans, and his blonde hair pulled back in a ponytail, Stills happily bounded into the radio control room, and shook hands all around. Among those in the studio was Mike Turney, a local kid who had wormed his way in with a stack of dog-eared Buffalo Springfield vinyl albums, hoping to snag an autograph.

"Where'd you get these?" Stills grinned, looking at the old albums like museum pieces. He obliged Turney by signing a couple of album jackets. Stills sat down behind the broadcast console and began writing down the names of rock 'n 'roll songs he wanted to play. He went back to his roots: rock 'n 'roll from the 1950s.

"Classic rock: It's got a good beat, it's got some meat to lyrics, and you can dance to it real good. Classic rock turns into Jurassic rock, and we don't want that," he said. "Speed-O" by the Cadillacs and "Yackety Yak" by the Coasters were some of the songs Stills selected.

"I've found the mother lode, I've found 'Speed-O,'" Stills exclaimed. Stills modestly declined to play any of his songs.

"I've heard me," he said. "You can play me after I'm gone."

Stills spent his time playing the old favorites and talking to fans who called. One fan seemed overwhelmed to be talking to Stills.

"Compose yourself son, it's all right. I'm just another dude," Stills said.

When he wasn't spinning records and talking to fans, he put in frequent plugs for his pet causes, including environmental protection. Asked about the view that rock was dead, Stills vigorously disagreed. "They have been trying to kill it for years. I'll bop until I drop," he said. But he despaired at what he called musical apartheid in the country, saying there is no crossover anymore. What makes a good song? The ingredients are in country music: cars, beer and lost love, he said.

That night, Stills played for a crowd in Daytona Beach. This time he was dressed in a suit with an open collar shirt and looked freshly scrubbed. He greeted me and said, "Hey Jim, I clean up pretty good don't I?"

In 1998, Kim and I got a chance to meet someone else that Ringo Starr, Stephen Stills, and the rest of the world, looked to as a founding pioneer of rock and roll.

Bo Diddley. Bo was known for his rectangular guitar, African beat, and the hits "I'm a Man" and "Bo Diddley." Then living in Archer, Fla., Bo came to Daytona Beach to perform for firefighters after a series of devastating wildfires torched thousands of acres in Florida.

Bo had a belief that everyone should give back to society if they have enjoyed success in their life and came as a favor to Gov. Lawton Chiles. Unlike some concerts where the venues are so huge that spectators can hardly see the performers, Bo performed on a little stage on the infield of Daytona Beach International Speedway. Firefighters were all around him as he played his hits. Afterward, he patiently signed autographs for anyone who wanted one. I got a great picture of Bo with Chiles onstage. The governor's office later contacted me and asked for a copy. I was happy to oblige.

My best rock and roll experience? No, but close.

The best would be a couple of interviews with Yoko Ono. Flip the page. That's the next chapter.

33 – Yoko

When The Beatles broke up in 1970, their fans were in disbelief. Disappointed, saddened, and pissed that the guys who had made so much magic would go their own ways. I vowed to never buy any of their solo albums. Not until they reunited, anyway. Surely, they

Yoko Ono sent this signed card to me in 1997. It was the first of several that I received from her. I especially liked the fact that the image showed John and Yoko's bed in for peace, surrounded by inquiring reporters just like me.

would have to get back together, wouldn't they? I kept that vow until the summer of 1973, when I broke down and bought John Lennon's "Mind Games." I was missing The Beatles, and Lennon in particular. They had always seemed so cosmically tuned into the swirling currents of the universe. Randomly, I picked "Mind Games" out of a bin in the record department at the Fort Gordon, Ga., post exchange. I had no idea what to expect. As soon as I got home and placed the album on the turntable, I was immediately smitten by the sound flowing out of my Sansui speakers. I was taken by the majesty and idealism of the soaring title track "Mind Games," as well as by the buoyant optimism of "Intuition," and the seditious nature of "Bring on the Lucie."

My affinity for Lennon and his iconoclastic views might seem out of step with what you would expect of an Army officer in 1973. There is a part of me that is nonconformist, and somehow manages to coexist with the orderly, diligent side. There is nothing that says I can't appreciate a rare genius like Lennon. What I particularly liked on Lennon's "Mind Games" album is the song "Out the Blue." John sings beautifully of the awe he felt at Yoko coming so unexpectedly into his life and the all-consuming passion that followed. The song begins with a gentle strumming of the guitar playing behind John's plaintive, sensitive, singing, building in power and emotion as piano, drums, bass, and a chorus, credited as "Something Different," are added to the mix. The emotional impact rivals the Righteous Brother's version of "Unchained Melody," and arguably surpasses it because the song is not about just any woman. It's about Yoko Ono. Maybe I identify so much with "Out the Blue" because John mirrors my own feelings about the miracle of finding and marrying Kim. To me, there was a parallel element of bridging the east-west divide, as well as the racial, religious, and cultural differences.

Was the impossible romance between Kim and me, born out of the Vietnam War, so different than the one between Yoko and John? Maybe not, if you take away their wealth and fame. Yoko herself might agree. Take a listen to her song "We're All Water."

I met and fell in love with Kim in 1969, while serving in Vietnam — the same year that John and Yoko married. Lennon made headlines campaigning for peace, while I was just one of the half million Americans in Vietnam, hoping to stay alive and return home. When a Beatles song played on the Armed Forces Vietnam Network that year, it might have been "Hey Jude" from 1968, or maybe "Get Back" from '69. I can't say that I ever heard Lennon's "Give Peace a Chance" in Vietnam. Understandably so. It wasn't what the generals wanted the grunts in the field to be listening to.

Over the years after I bought "Mind Games" in 1973, I bought all of the other solo albums by Lennon, those released in his lifetime and those released posthumously. I enjoyed them as much as I had his earlier Beatles' work. Sometimes even more so. And I bought most of the albums by the other former Beatles as well. Vinyl albums, tapes, compact discs, you name it. Much to the bemusement of Kim who sees all the boxes of records and wonders about my obsession. Lennon came closest in his solo career to matching what The Beatles had done, if you consider his greatest songs, his wry commentary, and his unique way of stirring the pot. That's just my opinion. I'm not denying that Paul, George, and Ringo didn't have their moments. I never got to see Lennon in a live performance. Or George Harrison for that matter.

So, suppose the opportunity arose to interview Lennon's muse, Yoko Ono, the controversial artist credited with co-writing "Imagine?" She intrigued and challenged Lennon and attracted the scorn and hatred of many fans for "breaking up The Beatles." It seemed like an impossibility with Yoko sitting in New York within the fortress walls of the Dakota. I wouldn't even presume to wish for such a thing.

The closest I had come to communicating with Yoko was in the 1990s, when I wrote her a letter of appreciation — a fan letter — and to my amazement received a signed card and a promo CD of her song "Listen the Snow is Falling," that she was sending as a Christmas card. I especially liked the fact that the signed card showed John and Yoko's bed in for peace, surrounded by inquiring reporters, just like me.

Over the next few years, I received several other signed cards from her. But the cards stopped when I took a new job in Bradenton, and I gave no thought to interviewing her. Then — you could almost say out of the blue — I got to interview Yoko Ono. Twice.

Once in 2007, and again in 2011, both times for the Bradenton Herald. Yoko was phoning in to newspapers where the traveling Lennon art exhibit of erotic lithographs and whimsical sketches made a stop, basically to drum up interest in the show. Sarasota was on the tour list. The assignment to interview Yoko was tossed

162

my way because of my reputation of being the newsroom Beatles nut. Even after all these years, Yoko still evokes strong feelings.

"Yewww, you're not interviewing her are you?" a co-worker at the Bradenton Herald said, wrinkling her nose, when she heard that our features editor had asked me if I wanted to interview Yoko.

"Oh yes," I responded. "You mean you wouldn't?"

At the appointed day and hour, an aide from Studio One in New York City called and told me my 15 minutes to talk to Yoko were about to begin. What should I call her? I wondered. A moment later, we started.

"Hello Yoko," I said, without hesitation.

Thus began the interview. She was nothing like her dragon lady mystique. She was friendly, funny, and self-deprecating. She patiently answered all my questions. I had much to ask Yoko, who has been immortalized in the "The Ballad of John and Yoko" and so many other songs.

Yoko, how about that nude "Two Virgins" album cover, the bed-ins for peace, and your book, "Grapefruit." Where did you find the courage? I asked.

She responded in a way that only Yoko can.

"I wasn't being brave at all," she said. "I was having a conversation with the universe."

In 2007, I asked Yoko about her favorite Beatles and John songs. She replied "All You Need is Love" and "Imagine," both iconic paeans to peace.

In 2011, I asked again what her favorites were. This time she said "Scared" from the 1974 album "Walls and Bridges," and "I'm Losing You," from the last album released in John's lifetime, "Double Fantasy." Both songs were full of the famous Lennon angst and insecurity.

"It's very gritty and one of the best," Yoko said of "I'm Losing You."

The album Double Fantasy is best known for its warm vision of happy family domesticity with John and Yoko taking the lead on alternating tracks. At the time of its release, a lot of people were unhappy that the album wasn't all John, considering that he hadn't been heard from in five years. Nevertheless, the album spoke to me and my life with Kim. Yes, we had missed the sexual revolution, the hippie lifestyle, and mind-altering drug use. But it seemed to me that the Lennons had eventually arrived at the same place we were. Home sweet home was the mantra of Double Fantasy. It was clear to me she never stopped carrying the torch for Lennon, whether it is his art, his music, or his books, and looking after his legacy. All too soon my 15 minutes with Yoko were up, and we said our goodbyes.

I'll never forget those interviews, although it's doubtful that Yoko remembers either of them. Several years later, I was talking to an Army Officer Candidate School friend, about the accomplishments of some of our classmates. I couldn't resist mentioning I had interviewed Yoko, because I was pretty confident that whatever my old OCS classmates had accomplished, none had interviewed Yoko.

He didn't miss a beat.

"Did you ask her why she broke up the Beatles?" Richard Green asked me.

34 - Fred

After we left Vietnam, we kept in touch with Fred and Hanh Freund who had been our good friends in Saigon. We were always grateful that they helped provide a support system for Kim and me as we worked through the red tape to get married during the war.

Kim with Fred Freund in Long Binh, Dec. 14, 1970.

Over the years, we visited them in Parsippany, N.J., Baltimore, Md., Whitestone, N.Y., and in Boca Raton, Fla. They came to our son's graduation from college, and we attended the wedding for their oldest daughter, Debbie, and the graduation from college of their youngest, Dorit. It was at about the time that Dorit graduated from the University of Florida, that I noticed a change in Fred. He seemed withdrawn, and depressed, nothing like the younger man I had known in Vietnam. Even so, I could always snap him out of it, for a few moments at least, by asking him a provocative question about politics in America. He was a keen observer of the never-ending political turmoil, and current events in the world, and frequently wrote letters to his local newspaper. He would passionately argue his position. Not until many years later did I began to understand what was eating at Fred.

The answer is found in an unfinished manuscript that he began working on a couple of years before his death, and then put aside. Fred could never escape the horror of the Holocaust and what it did to his family. His father fled the Nazis in Germany in 1938, and his mother followed a year later, after 14 failed escape attempts. For a while the Freunds lived an underground existence in Brussels, hiding from the constant threat of deportations to concentration camps.

"A family totally separated, living in harsh war times and persecution living conditions — children without parents and siblings separated, too. I was barely seven years old and my sister barely 10-years-old when our holocaust survival ordeal began in France," Fred wrote.

As a young child, he and his family escaped Belgium on a cattle train that was staffed by the Luftwaffe before it entered France. The first stop was at an empty chateau in Vallons-en-Sully, where the Freunds were housed in horse stables and slept on straw mattresses. Fred's father was snatched up for work in a labor battalion of foreign workers, and later escaped deportation to a concentration camp by leaping from a train. Fred and his sister did not see their father again for three years. Fred, his sister, and mother next stopped at a refugee community center in Limoges, France, and then went into hiding to escape French and German authorities who were trying to sweep up Jews to send to concentration camps. For a while, Fred and his sister were in hiding together with a French farm family, then were separated, and sent to separate Catholic orphanages.

"The Catholic orphanage was the most traumatic experience for me: a Jewish child with a hidden identity reciting the rosary in daily masses. It was a lonely, miserable life but my life was saved. The hiding in the Catholic orphanage was not too long. Salvation
166

was at hand guided by hidden guardian angels," Fred wrote. In late 1943, Fred and his sister were reunited with their mother and father near Grenoble.

"A new family life started from us. I even had to relearn German from my parents to communicate with them," he said. The Freunds stayed in a six-story building, a converted convent with eight refugee families living on each floor.

"Living was very modest with bare necessities — food was meager and there was constant fear of French police and German actions to seize Jews for deportation before liberation by the U.S. Army in southern France, Fred wrote. Every weekend we begged and scavenged for food in the countryside from French farmers — eggs, milk, vegetables, grains for milling. Some farmers were generous, other farmers were stingy and sometimes hostile. Thus, we could never know what food we would have to nourish ourselves. I can still remember a gentle French farmer saying to us, 'So young and already Jewish.' We really were strangers to the French farmers. We were a family again, although we lived in constant fear. We had false identities as Polish refugees. We were malnourished. I suffered from ulcers for many years thereafter. Our entire family suffered for six agonizing years. The joy of liberation did not come soon enough to stop the atrocities committed by the Germans who were fighting the French resistance in our area. Resistance members were hanged in Voreppe which was only a few miles south of LaBuisse on the route to Grenoble. A dozen limp bodies were hanging on trees at the entrance to the village — a horrifying public revenge hanging by German sadists. The Germans even stopped and killed Jews in retreat." After the end of World War II, the Freund family moved to Palestine in 1945.

"We lived through the entire Israel independence and state building period. We left Israel in 1954 with new German citizenship for a two-year stay in Berlin primarily to take care of compensation paid by the German government. My parents and sisters received indemnity compensations and lifetime pensions. I received a one-time retroactive compensation for poor health."

Fred lamented that he did not receive lifetime payments like his other family members.

167

Fred Freund smiles with a boot of beer on his 80th birthday as Chin Klein and I show him some love.

"I had a severe depression in 1991 that was attributed to Holocaust suffering. I had several relapses in following years with a current relapse now." In 1956, the Freunds moved to the United States, where Fred studied electrical engineering, and graduated summa cum laude from City College of New York. I met Fred in Saigon in 1969, while he was working for IBM performing computer work for the Military Assistance Command Vietnam. He was a computer pioneer, and he never really stopped working in that field until his death in 2016 at age 82.

There exists a bit of Super 8 movie film from 1971 outside Fred's rented house in the Gia Dinh section of Saigon, that shows Kim and I holding hands and walking across a courtyard. A mischievous little girl, Fred's daughter Debbie, runs by and I scoop her up and place her on my shoulders. Fred was the photographer. On the next segment, I am the photographer, and I capture a tender moment between Fred and Hanh as he brushes back a wayward strand of her hair. Hanh is holding their newborn

168

daughter Dorit, and Debbie is there, too, jumping up and down. Even now, this little bit of film, and Barbra Streisand singing "Memories" can just about bring me to tears. When Fred turned 80, ironically on another day that now lives in infamy, Sept. 11, we drove over to Boca Raton to do whatever he wanted on his birthday.

What Fred wanted was to go to a good German restaurant, and have a meal with German beer. We did. It was a great night, and it was the first time that any of us had ever seen him have a beer. He never stopped surprising us. Even with the horror of the Holocaust, he was able to separate the Nazi's evil deeds from an even longer and more enduring benevolent German legacy personified by Johann Wolfgang von Goethe, Martin Luther, Ludwig von Beethoven and Johann Sebastian Bach.

Fred and I became good friends and he taught me many things, including how to play chess, although I could never hope to beat him. His analytical mind was always thinking too many moves ahead for me. Maybe even more importantly, Fred offered an example of how to live bravely, even defiantly, in an often cruel and indifferent world.

35 – Jeb

I've talked to all kinds of people in the Army and in the newspaper business. Many were remarkable in their own way, even though most were not celebrities, nor were they famous outside their own neighborhood.

Jeb Bush in 1998 at Daytona International Speedway. A month later he was elected governor of Florida. (Photo by the author)

One conversation I'll never forget was about 6:30 p.m. in late November 1995, as I was laying out the next edition of the New Smyrna Beach Observer. It had been a long day, and there were several more hours of work before I would go home. Suddenly, there was Jeb Bush on the line, apologizing for the rude treatment

I had received at Presidency III, the Republican Straw Poll held in Orlando a couple of weeks earlier and telecast on CNN. I had taken my daughter Christine, who even as a young girl loved baseball and politics, to the Straw Poll to watch the process. Several times during the Straw Poll, over-zealous volunteers had rudely ordered me to "sit down," "stand back," and "go outside, and we'll talk about it." I was nowhere close to a candidate, nor was I impeding business. But I knew there was no future in arguing with an over-zealous volunteer drunk on their own power. Each time I did as I was told. But it rankled, and I mentioned the abuse to one of the folks I knew from Volusia County. I told her that I understood the difficulty of managing several thousand attendees and ensuring security for seven or eight presidential candidates. But there is a right way to do things and a wrong way.

I pretty much forgot about the incident until I got that call from Jeb Bush from his home in Dade County. Bush apologized and said he had heard several similar complaints. He knew me from several visits to New Smyrna Beach when he was running for governor against Lawton Chiles. I had first met Bush several years earlier, when he had visited a couple in their New Smyrna home. In those days, he was very thin, had movie star good looks, and in his suit had an Ivy League vibe going. I remembered being impressed by his good manners and quiet demeanor. At the time, he had not been elected to any office.

Bush told me that everyone, media or not, deserves to be treated with respect and diplomacy. He was sincere, friendly, matter of fact. At the time of the phone call, Bush was still licking his wounds after losing the gubernatorial election to Chiles. I asked him about a controversial blitz of last-minute phone calls, 1.1 million of them, just before the election that were funded by the Chiles campaign. The callers falsely accused Bush of being a tax cheat, and said that his running mate, Tom Feeney, wanted to abolish Social Security and cut Medicare.

Chiles later apologized for the calls and said his top campaign officials were to blame. I asked Bush if he took any solace in the closeness of the race, considering the impact that those phone calls might have made. Bush refused to make any excuses or express any bitterness.

"If our message had been stronger," Bush said, his campaign would have succeeded.

Bush shouldered the blame for the loss and refused to pass the buck. His stock rose in my book. He was later elected governor, and came to be regarded by Floridians as one of the state's best governors. Bush didn't need to make a call to a small-town newspaper editor on a Wednesday evening. It wasn't necessary. It wasn't expected. But he did, which told me a lot about the man. He reinforced the power of three little words that can be so difficult to say: I am sorry. I always felt that Jeb Bush's loss to Lawton Chiles in his first gubernatorial run cost him a shot at the presidency. He was the best of the Bush brothers, yet it was his brother George W., who became president. By the time Jeb decided to run in 2016, he had been out-of-office too long, was out of shape for a campaign run. Like all the other GOP candidates, he was demolished by Donald Trump in the primaries.

Jeb Bush was not "low energy" like Trump said. His ship had unfortunately sailed years earlier.

36 - Citizen Kim

Citizen Kim at the Orange County Convention Center in Orlando in 1994.

Kim had not seen her family in Vietnam for nearly two decades. There were big barriers to such a visit. Until the mid-1990s, there were no diplomatic relations between the United States and Vietnam. Kim's passport was defunct. It had been issued by the Republic of Vietnam, more commonly known as the government of the defeated South Vietnam. As a first step, in 1989 Kim applied for U.S. citizenship. It would be — what else — a struggle. So, it always seems with us.

At that time, the Immigration and Naturalization Service was taking anywhere from 18 months to two years to process a citizenship application. We received no response from INS in two years of waiting. We wrote several letters to the INS which went unanswered. It was hard for this born-and-bred American to keep a rein on his emotions. Why wasn't my government responding to me? We wrote to U.S. Rep. Craig James, who in turn wrote a letter to the INS on our behalf. James also failed to get a response. In 1992, James announced he was retiring from Congress. Two heavyweights raised their hands to replace him: John Mica and Dan Webster.

Frankly, when it came time for our newspaper editorial board to endorse a candidate, I took the measure of both men, and chose the one who I thought would provide the most effective constituent service. In my mind, that was Mica. I never said a word to Mica about my problem, but after he won, and settled into office, I wrote him a letter as John Q. Citizen, rather than as Mr. Editor. Mica's staff discovered that the INS had our letters in a file, as well as the one from Craig James, but could not find that anyone from INS had ever responded. We resubmitted the application with Mica's office closely following its progress.

At the end of 1993, Kim received a notice to report to Orlando for a hearing on her application. She would be quizzed on her knowledge of the Constitution and U.S. history, as well as any aspects of her personal history that the examiner wanted to know more about. We spent more time looking for the INS office than Kim spent during the hearing. She got the examiner's stamp of approval, and a date for taking the oath.

In 1994, Kim and 256 other people representing 55 countries took the oath of citizenship at the Orange County Convention Center in Orlando. David Angotti, the Immigration and Naturalization official who administered the oath, afterward had each person clinch their fist, punch the sky and shout "Yes!" Then he had them to turn around and congratulate a new citizen of the United States.

Dan, Christine, and I watched proudly from the back of the room, the closest we could get with that overflow crowd. Seeing that big smile on her face, made all the frustration seem to melt away. We had no hard feelings toward the INS. The glitch was just one of those things. The citizenship ceremony was conducted with dignity, celebrating the solemnity and importance of the day. With her citizenship certificate, Kim received all the rights that Americans take for granted: the right to vote, to serve on juries, and to travel with a U.S. passport.

That was a good year. Our son Dan was working on a civil engineering degree to go with the electrical engineering degree he had already earned. Christine finished her associate of arts. There were some fun things, too, in 1994. I got to photograph the Rolling Stones up close in Gainesville during their Voodoo Lounge tour, I had been elected president-elect of the chamber of commerce in New Smyrna Beach, and had set a personal best time in the six-mile run, at age 48. More importantly, with U.S.-Vietnam relations improving in the 1990s, we hoped that Kim, a new American citizen, might soon be able to return to the land of her birth. The final piece of the puzzle fell into place, when I won a corporate cash prize for a progress edition that we published in New Smyrna Beach, enough money to allow Kim to go back to Vietnam to see the family she had not seen in nearly 25 years.

In 1997, she at last returned to Vietnam. There was nobody there to greet her when she arrived in Ho Chi Minh City, the former Saigon. Her family didn't know she was coming. She showed up unannounced in Bac Lieu and was warmly welcomed home by her astonished family. I wasn't there, of course, but I celebrated the homecoming from afar.

In 1999, Dan, now grown to a full 6-foot-1, and working as an electrical engineer in California, took his wife, Xuan, baby daughter Amanda, and his mother, Kim, back to Vietnam. It was his first trip back since 1973. It was a nearly perfect visit, until one of the party misplaced her travel documents on the way home. There was no way they were returning to the United States without her, so they missed their flight and checked into a hotel. The travelers were fast running out of money, saved only by the cash that Kim had stashed away. I helped the best I could with phone calls from Bradenton, where I had gone to work for the Bradenton Herald.

After a few anxious days, the American consulate in Ho Chi Minh City helped get their paperwork in order, allowing the travelers to return to the United States. We never did figure out how those travel documents were lost.

While I was thrilled for Kim for being able to visit Vietnam with Dan and his family, there was something I wanted to do. I wanted to go back to Vietnam with her.

37 - Floyd

Hurricane Floyd was a massive brute of a storm that skirted the east coast of Florida in August 1999.

Even though Floyd missed New Smyrna Beach and all of Florida, and finally made landfall in the Carolinas, it got me thinking about my career.

There was an incident during Floyd that would have been funny, if it hadn't been so disapointing.

While most of the newspaper staff decided to evacuate the area, I told management I would ride it out and report to the office in the morning to put out the next edition.

I was shocked when I reported to work the next day with storm photos and notes, ready to go work.

I found a hand-written note on my desk from the manager they, too, had evacuated the area.

The only staff member on company property was me, and I could not produce the paper and run the press, too.

It was the only time in my career that a newspaper I was associated with missed an issue.

Taking a hard look at what I had accomplished in 14 years in New Smyrna Beach, I knew that I was overdue to make a change.

Quietly, I began sending out resumes. Almost immediately, I got a response from Joanne Mamenta, managing editor of the Bradenton Herald. I was impressed with how nice she was, and all the jobs that were available.

"Do you want to be an editor or a reporter?" she asked.

I thought it over.

"I can do every job in the newsroom. I am an editor," I told Mamenta. "I don't want to start over as a reporter."

It wasn't a boast. It was the truth.

I drove over to Bradenton on a Saturday, and met Executive Editor Joan Krauter, who was in her office on her day off, casually dressed in sandals, shorts and a blouse, as she wrapped a gift for a bridal shower. I could see that she loved the business, was a serious journalist, and could probably teach me a thing or two. Most importantly, I liked her.

The back door of Council's Pool Room, where the best burgers in Bradenton are served.

My primary assignment that day was to edit a long, overwritten story on a developer who had circumvented the rules for getting certificates of occupancy. It was an easy story to edit and improve. I declined to stay a second day, reasoning that the editors at the Bradenton Herald should have seen enough to either want me or not.

I drove back to New Smyrna Beach, wondering whether I really wanted to leave the job I had held for more than 14 years. Then I received an invitation to drive down to Florida Today in Melbourne for an interview.

Suddenly, I had two offers to consider.

Ultimately, I rejected Florida Today because I thought I would clash with their metro editor. They had too many editors running around in white shirts and ties (I had always despised ties). And then there was the giant bust of the head of Al Neuharth, founder of USA Today, in the front lobby. It seemed the sculpture was nearly almost as large as Neuharth's famous ego.

I told Joan that I would be happy to accept her offer, even if she did want me to start as the night metro editor. I had applied for a job as day editor, but the night editor had resigned before my arrival, leaving a critical vacancy.

There was also an opening for a metro editor at the Bradenton Herald. I gave Joan a lead, which she used to fill that position.

Ironically, the Bradenton Herald and Today were newspapers that I had unsuccessfully applied to in 1977, when I was trying to break into the business. Many of the reporters who had stormed newsrooms in the months and years after Watergate, gobbling up the good jobs in a quest to become the next Woodward and Bernstein, had gone on to greener pastures. Now they were in public relations, marketing, and government information jobs.

In late 1999, I made a career change, moving 180 miles away from New Smyrna Beach via Interstate 4 to Florida's west coast and the Bradenton Herald. It was the most difficult move I had ever made.

When I said goodbye to the Observer's staff it felt like I was saying goodbye to my children. I felt terrible about leaving them and all the friends that I had made in town.

Making the move even more difficult was the fact that Kim stayed in New Smyrna Beach. Our daughter, Christine, was still living at home, and Kim didn't want to leave her. Like she always said: the kids are number-one, you're number-two. A final consideration was that my mother lived near New Smyrna Beach. It was an agonizing move.

Some in New Smyrna Beach wondered why I would leave a job as executive editor and accept a job as assistant metro editor. Wasn't that a demotion? No, I would answer, because the Bradenton Herald was a much larger newspaper, and had more upside career potential.

The Bradenton Herald had resources I could only dream about. There were 63 staff members in the newsroom. The New Smyrna Beach Observer had six or seven.

What I didn't tell my friends in New Smyrna was that I feared for the viability of The Observer, and that I was underpaid. I knew that if I wanted to make more money, I would have to move.

For the first three years I was in Bradenton, I rented a room from my Aunt Gena during the week and drove back to New Smyrna Beach every weekend. It would have been exhausting had I allowed myself to think about it.

People would ask me, "Is your marriage OK?"

"I love my wife, the marriage has never been stronger," I would say.

A little more than a year after moving to Bradenton, I was named East Manatee editor, responsible for coverage of the county's fastest-growing area. I held that job from 2001 until I retired, sort of, in 2013.

In 2002, the Bradenton Herald named me employee of the year. That was in part because of Joan's encouragement and support, but also because I shouldered my responsibilities the same as if I owned the company.

Each week, Mac Tully, publisher at the time, would bring the Herald's directors to the East Manatee newsroom for a briefing on how we were doing versus our competition. I could demonstrate that we were decisively beating our competition in terms of breaking news and story count.

Tully asked what worried me most.

"Everything," I told him.

It turned out that was the correct answer.

180

In Bradenton, I found not only a new lease on a career, but enjoyment in the work that made it a pleasure. I was able to work with other reporters and editors, and also write and photograph at will, helping to capture the heart and character of a community.

Working with Joan could be a challenge.

"It's like you would jump as high as you could on a story, and she would hold a stick up and say, jump a little higher," I would tell reporters.

But she had a fine ability to see holes in a story, and questions that had not been asked. Inevitability, her editorial sense could help make any story better.

There would be adventures, too, that could not be had anywhere else, including riding in a Coast Guard hurricane hunter across the Gulf of Mexico, looking for signs of oil from the Deepwater Horizon disaster or flying in a 1929 Ford Trimotor plane across Sarasota Bay.

Also coming to mind are the once-in-a-lifetime experience of riding in President George W. Bush's motorcade and covering President Barack Obama during two visits to the area.

I found that Bradenton's people and institutions were as interesting and quirky as any place I had worked. A favorite: Council's Pool Room, where they serve their hamburgers on a napkin, and often with some guff from the owner about something he disliked in the newspaper. But don't ask for fries because they weren't on the menu.

I will always be grateful to Joan, the last in a line of great women who made a difference in my life. Grateful that she gave me a job, that she appreciated my work, and that she became my friend.

Finally, in 2003, Kim and I bought a house in Bradenton and Kim made the move to Florida's west coast. About the same time, the New Smyrna Beach Observer failed and shuttered its doors. It confirmed for me that if I was going to stay in the newspaper business, I had to make that move to another town in 1999.

I refused to work for my old competition, the Daytona Beach News-Journal. While the News-Journal offered me a job, I would have felt like a hypocrite taking it, considering how many years we had slugged it out.

38 - No words

*My mother with her last husband, Harry, in a Welaka, Fla.,
hayfield. This photo says a lot about their relationship and her
joy in living in the rural village along the Saint Johns River.*

It seemed that every time I made a career move, I lost a loved one.
It happened in 1977 when I went to work in Clewiston, and my
great-grandmother, Maggie Butler died. Slightly more than a year
after moving to New Smyrna Beach in 1985, my father died. And
then about 18 months after moving to Bradenton in 1999, I lost my
mother. Coincidences for sure, but sad markers all the same.

It was a bad year — 2001 — when my mother died. A few months
later, there was the terrorist attacks of 9/11, and then early in
2002, my stepfather, Harry, died from Alzheimer's Disease, and
my little brother, Tony, died after a long struggle with brain
cancer. My mother, Thelma Louise Johnson, had a rough life,
although you would never know it to talk to her. She was chatty,
and full of love for her children. She was a great hostess, who
enjoyed cooking for us, and welcomed our friends into her home
like they were family. She liked bling, a dirty joke, little brown
cigarettes, and a mixed drink, or a beer.

She was a consistent cheerleader and morale booster for me when
I was in Vietnam.

In October 1970, I came home from Vietnam on 30-day leave, and
my mother pulled together a welcome home party, with uncles and

aunts, my grandmother, and great-grandmother attending, and my dad and stepmother, too. The party was held at her little house on Nelms Street in a quiet neighborhood of Jacksonville. The ghosts of the past had finally been put to rest. I returned to

Thelma Louise Johnson, about the time she threw a party for me and my brother-in-law, Jim Presnell in 1970. We were both Vietnam vets.

Vietnam after that leave, and two months later, Kim and I were married in an Army chapel in Long Binh. When Kim and I left Vietnam in June of 1971, my mother, and my sisters Phyllis and Sandi were there to greet us at the airport in Jacksonville. It was one of the happiest days of my life to finally be able to introduce Kim to my family.

Thelma sometimes questioned her maternal instincts, and years later volunteered that she regretted leaving my father. One of my sisters said our mother wasn't a traditional milk-and-cookies mom. But she was cool, and she was fun to be around. She made great biscuits, too. When I was about four years old, I turned over a cabinet trying to reach a plate of hot biscuits and broke every plate and glass in the house. They were that good. I miss those biscuits, but I miss her even more. We are never ready to say goodbye to our mothers.

***

As difficult as it was to say goodbye to Thelma, fate dealt the family another blow less than a year later when my little brother Tony died of brain cancer. When my father and Margie married in 1959, she brought two little girls, Nancy and Kathy, and a beautiful baby boy named Tony into the family. Tony immediately became the family favorite. As soon as the little blond toddler began to talk, he would introduce himself as, "Hi, I Tony."

I was nearly a teenager when Tony came into the family, so it was my job to frighten him with ghost noises in the night, and a little later to teach him to throw and catch a football. He grew into a

Tony

handsome boy, played running back on his junior high school football team, where he was named captain.

In high school, upper level girls would come to pick him up on dates. Fortunately, his good looks were balanced by a good heart, and a fun sense of humor. Our sisters, all five of them, liked to pin him to the floor and tickle him, even after he was fully grown. Kim loved Tony, too, and would join in the tickling. Tony shadowed our father in the garage and might easily have become a mechanic. He learned how to tear down and repair engines as a teenager, that's how smart he was. But instead he became a top-notch salesman and sales manager. When his sales route took him to New Smyrna Beach, he would always stop by the newsroom and give me a big hug and the latest family news.

One time, Tony sent my newspaper a letter to the editor about me and my military service, but I short-stopped it, because I couldn't have my family bragging about me like that in print. But I kept the letter, because it reflected Tony's personality so well.

"I will always remember, although I did not know why, standing in our living room with my family in tears the day my brother left," Tony wrote of when I went to Vietnam. "Little did I know what lay ahead for my brother and many others. My brother was one of the lucky ones that made it back home safely. We all cried together for the ones that did not."

Eventually Tony settled down and married Debbie Berg. They had three children. Then one Saturday morning while the kids were watching cartoons, Tony blacked out. When he regained consciousness, he drove himself to the hospital. Doctors discovered that he had a cancerous tumor deep in his brain. I held his hand just before he went into surgery. "You're going to be alright, I'll see you when you come out," I told Tony.

And for several years, he did seem to be OK, although his speech was never as quick as before, and sometimes he hesitated as he searched for a word. Tony fought cancer for 13 years, but sadly died in 2002, less than a year after my mother had passed away. Tony was brave throughout his illness. The day before his death, he told us he was at peace, and comforted by his faith. Tony was the best of us, and he was beloved. He had so few years but lived the years that he had to the fullest. Tony brought much joy and laughter to those who were fortunate to have known him. He will never be forgotten.

It was another reaffirmation that nothing lasts forever, and that love is all there is.

39 – Hello Vietnam

Lieu Thi Bay in 1971   *Lieu Thi Bay in 2006*

Spurred by recent family losses, and the realization that time waits for no one, in 2006, Kim and I returned to Vietnam together for the first time since 1971. Kim was excited and happy to soon be seeing her family again. I was happy for Kim but full of misgivings. Two days after our arrival in Ho Chi Minh City, the former Saigon, we were 140 miles south in Bac Lieu, in Kim's home village, and I was about to see her mother again for the first time in 35 years. A rented minibus dropped us off near a dirt alley off Highway 1. In the company of assorted nieces and nephews, we walked down the alley past a Vietnamese army medical detachment, to the Bac Lieu River.

There, I got separated from Kim as two of her nieces guided me onto a narrow boat — just about one-butt wide and riding just inches above the brown water of the Bac Lieu River. A boatman rowed us across the river, a five-minute paddle, and we climbed up the opposite shore to a tree-lined path. With Kim still on the other shore, the two nieces, young women about 18 or 19, guided me into a quiet house on the riverbank. I entered, speaking little Vietnamese, and Kim's nieces speaking no English.

I saw my mother-in-law, Lieu Thi Bay, sitting up in bed. She was 85, unable to walk after breaking a hip several years earlier. I knelt at her side and took her hand. My eyes filled with tears. The last time I had seen her was shortly before I left Vietnam with Kim in 1971.

"Chao Me," I said, greeting her in Vietnamese with "Hello Mother." "Me manh khong?" I said, asking how she was doing, and just about exhausting my knowledge of Vietnamese.

"Me manh," she replied, her eyes twinkling as she squeezed my hand, indicating she was fine. I was consumed with guilt for taking her daughter away all those years ago. Communications after the war had been difficult for many years. I sensed that I was welcome in her home. The awkward moment had passed, if not a giant lump in my throat.

We had all aged so much.

In 1971, Lieu Thi Bay was care-worn from years of poverty and war stress. But she was dignified, then and now. I could see where Kim got her beauty. Maybe it was a miracle Lieu Thi Bay had survived for so long, through so much trouble and danger. Now she was the matron of the family, beloved and respected by a host of children, grandchildren, and great-grandchildren. I held Lieu Thi Bay's hand until Kim arrived a few minutes later. When mother and daughter were reunited, there were tears, laughter and embraces. I watched the release of years of emotion

I stood back and enjoyed the reunion. The journey had been hard, but those first moments, filled with joy, touched the heart in a profound way. We were home.

***

No question, the Vietnam War is the defining event in my life. I won't speak for the rest of my generation but I know many of them feel the same way.

There was a quiet life before the war, as I moved from high school, and into the work place. Then I found myself swept up by this vast rip current of history, changing my life in ways that I could not have imagined.

When Kim and I returned together to Vietnam in early 2006, the emotion was overwhelming. We were returning to the deadly, tumultuous place of our youth, when we joined our fortunes and bravely, if naively, stepped into the future.

We stopped to say prayers at a temple in Tra Kha Villag that Kim's family helped start.

The communists, the descendants of the Viet Cong and the North Vietnamese Army were in charge in Vietnam, and I wondered how I would react to them. And how they would react to me. I worried about that as we flew into Vietnam, in brilliant sunshine, so different from the midnight darkness of 1968, when I arrived at Bien Hoa with a planeload of other American troops. It seemed so peaceful, as our airliner neared Ho Chi Minh City, near the end of a punishing 24-hour flight over the Pacific Ocean. Concerns included a bird flu outbreak, and the threat of malaria. Also, I worried about my status as retired U.S. soldier and still working journalist who was in Vietnam on family vacation. Would that set off alarms at Tan Son Nhut Airport? And what about Kim's family? How would they react to me?

188

Most of the passengers on that plane were Vietnamese, who had fled their homeland after the war. They were labeled "Viet Kieu," Vietnamese living in America. They acted different than their brothers and sisters who had stayed in Vietnam. They moved differently, dressed differently, had more money than those they had left behind. As we neared Tan Son Nhut, the passengers moved to the the land side of the plane to watch their homeland emerge. Not only would they be reunited with families, they would be celebrating Tet, the lunar New Year. The holiday is a big deal, something like rolling our Christmas, Thanksgiving and New Year into one.

Kim, right, walks down a Saigon street with a cousin.

As the plane touched down, the passengers applauded, just like the G.I.s had done years ago when their chartered airliners left Vietnam for the United States.When the plane landed at Tan Son Nhut Airport, we got in line to pass through immigration, manned by young men in army uniforms.

I had a moment of paranoia, seeing those uniforms, but quickly realized my apprehension was misplaced. Those officials weren't my enemies. They were not even born when I was in Vietnam from 1968 to 1971. The immigration official stamped my papers and waved me through. As I waited for Kim, I read a sign, asking travelers to do their outsourcing in Vietnam. What would Uncle

Ho have thought? After passing through the regimentation of customs, order seemed to break down as a mass of people tried to grab their luggage at once. Then order was restored as they got back into another line to clear customs.

Outside the terminal, there were hundreds of Vietnamese waiting for relatives to deplane. Nobody was there to greet us so we hailed a cab. Kim was worried that the cabbie might try to rob us.

"No worries, I can take him," I jokingly told Kim. Our drive to the hotel was uneventful.

***

This was not the Saigon I remembered. In the old days the streets were filled with bicycles and subcompact blue-and-white Renault taxis. Now, the same streets were packed with motorcycles, Mercedes-Benz buses, and Toyotas, which seemed to be in s perpetual horn honking mode. The bustling low-rise Saigon I remembered has been replaced by a bustling high-rise metropolis, and free enterprise was the order of the day. Except, there was the incongruity of the Vietnamese flag with its yellow star on a red background, and red banners with the communist hammer and sickle. As we neared our hotel, we saw a Soviet-made tank that made world headlines in 1975 by knocking down the gates of the presidential palace, signaling the end of the war. The tank was still parked on former president Thieu's the front lawn.

The image of the tank, and of refugees struggling to get to the rooftop of the U.S. Embassy for a helicopter flight to escape the advancing communists, remains indelibly locked in the minds of anyone who watched it on TV. During the Vietnam War, 3.4 million Americans served in Southeast Asia, and more than 58,000 lost their lives in the war. We discovered that even though the Vietnamese suffered horribly in that cruel war, most seemed to have the future on their minds, and were willing to extend a welcoming home to any American they might encounter.

We had been in Ho Chi Minh City for less than a day when members of Kim's family arrived in a rented Mercedes minibus to take us to Bac Lieu, the city of her birth. Two of her brothers, a sister, and several nieces and nephews greeted us in the lobby of the Hotel Oscar our first morning in Vietnam. Everyone grabbed a piece of luggage and threw it onto the minibus. We left immediately for Bac Lieu, six hours to the south down Highway 1. As the bus pulled out of town, we recognized old landmarks, including the opera house, but all of the old military strongpoints and barbed wire were gone. There were remnants of the old low-rise Saigon, decorated with holiday lights, new year wishes, such as "Chuc Mung Nam Moi," and images of the dog, whose year it was. And here, by coincidence, were we, too. I was born in the year of the dog (1946), and we were married in the year of the dog (1970). Our time in Vietnam seemed to be cosmically connected to years of the dog.

During the war, there were at least two ferries on Highway 1 between Saigon and Bac Lieu. But the one at Vinh Long had since been replaced by a modern suspension bridge. At Can Tho, a fleet of ferries still operated in 2006. Once we cleared the Bassac River in Can Tho, we began seeing endless rice fields of intense green. Our driver kept us on Highway 1, and someone pointed out a narrow lane that led to the airfield where my old unit, Company D, 52nd Signal Battalion had been located. We would take a day trip to Soc Trang, but not this day. I recognized almost nothing about Soc Trang. It was no longer a little village, but a mid-sized city with broad boulevards, and a jumble of businesses and homes along Highway 1. The next stop would be Bac Lieu, Kim's birthplace. Our impatience and excitement grew the closer we got.

Our first morning in Kim's home village, we walked a mile down a tree-shaded lane to the local marketplace. The lane followed the Bac Lieu River, where there was a steady putt-putt of engines from passing barges, fuel tankers, fishing boats and more. We stopped into a Buddhist temple near Kim's mother's house, lit incense and said a prayer. I prayed for my fellow Americans who died or were injured in the war, and also for the Vietnamese people, that they might have a better life. Vietnam is at peace now, but we felt an obligation to pray for deliverance after so much suffering and sacrifice. We were not just tourists. We had lived share of our lives during Vietnam's worst days. Kim told me later that her family had donated the land for this temple, and one other nearer central Back Lieu, that was founded in 1876.

In the bright light of day, Vietnam is a dazzling country with its energetic people, and daily bustle. The lane outside Lieu Thi Bay's house was lined with flowering bougainvillea, and tropical plants, including guava, coconut, and banana. And there were a few reminders of the past, including a tangle of U.S. Army field wire, WD-1, which the American Signal Corps, and the South Vietnamese army used to connect field phones with field switchboards. In Kim's village, the two-pair wire connected homes with the local telephone service and carried the signal for dial-up internet.

I felt like a minority of one as walked around Bac Lieu. I saw no other westerners. My presence so far from Saigon — the largest hub of tourism — inspired mostly surprise among the locals. Kim made sure a niece and nephew accompanied me wherever I went, and I enjoyed smiling and greeting the locals we passed along the way. Most returned my greeting, or even shook my hand. A few said nothing and looked away. A woman seated on the back of a motorcycle even blew me a kiss.

Kim's nephew Vu and her niece Thao accompanied me on many of my walks. Both were college students. Thao was studying food technology. Vu was studying the food export business. Both had aspirations to move on to bigger cities, maybe Can Tho or even Ho Chi Minh City. Surprisingly, after we got to know each other a little I learned that Vu and Thao spoke some English. Thao was the quieter of the two, and very shy. But she was also very smart. I could almost see the wheels moving when I asked her a question. She would consider her words, and then answer in a complete English sentence. We have stayed in touch in the years since, and I always tell her that she is my favorite niece.

Vu had a surprise for me, too. He pulled a newspaper photo of Bill Clinton out of his wallet and showed it to me. Vu said he admired Clinton as a peacemaker, and one who helped improve relations between Vietnam and the United States. One day we stopped at a roadside coffee shop, and the waitress handed me a tiny cup of very strong coffee. I was the first American she had ever served. On another occasion, I managed to go downtown on my own and

192

walk through several neighborhoods, where I ran into a retired schoolteacher named Tran Duc. He invited me into his house, which was made of tin sheets, and offered me a can of Coke. In the corner of the room was a live chicken under a basket. I was touched by his hospitality and friendliness. He didn't have much money, and he wasn't in the best of health. Duc wore very thick glasses and wrote his letters very large because his sight was very dim. He was curious about me and asked lots of questions about the United States. I thanked him for inviting me to visit and we promised to write each other after I returned to the United States.

My new friend Tran Duc, who I met in a stroll through a Bac Lieu neighborhood.

When I returned to Kim's mother's house, the family was in disbelief that I could go off by myself, make a new friend, and return home without help. "Tran Duc," one mused. "Yes I know Tran Duc." All I could say of my feat of independence and navigation is geography is geography. A smile and a little sense of direction doesn't hurt either.

40 - Back to Soc Trang

*U.S. bunkers from the Vietnam War were still standing at the old
Soc Trang Airfield in 2006.*

With the passage of time, and the tremendous growth of villages
into towns and cities, I didn't know where to start looking for Soc
Trang Airfield, where Company D, 52nd Signal Battalion had set up
shop back in the 1960s. There were rumors that the Soc Trang
airfield, built on a former World War II Japanese fighter base, had
fallen into disrepair, and was no longer in service. I wanted badly
to see what remained of the airfield, having spent the seven most
important months of my life there. It was there that I had been a
company commander, and where I had met Kim, and where I had
met unforgettable characters. They included an Air Force
lieutenant who was the airfield weather forecaster and one of my
first friends at Soc Trang, attack helicopter pilots with their Viking
mustaches, and dedicated lieutenants, sergeants and enlisted men
of Company D, 52nd Signal Battalion, doing their best so far from
home. My time as company commander at Soc Trang had been the

most challenging, rewarding, and consequential of my life. We rented a taxi and drove from Bac Lieu to Soc Trang.

After arriving in town, we learned that Soc Trang airfield was still an active Vietnamese military base, and we would be unable to visit. Post-war sprawl had replaced the rice fields that I remembered around the edges of the airfield. Stopping to buy fruit from a roadside vendor, we learned about another road that would take us on the opposite side of the airfield. Sure enough, the road took us along one side of the walled compound and we could see the rooftops inside. It might have been a college campus, except for the the U.S. Army's old concrete bunkers, still standing guard, battered and blacked.

Memories came rushing back of how I had waded into chest-deep water to set claymore mines in front of the bunkers manned by my company. I also recalled the two men from Company D who were wounded while standing guard duty one night during a mortar attack. I remembered the officers club at Soc Trang, where we might watch a movie, drink, or pull pranks on one another. Most of all, I remembered meeting the young woman who would become my wife and change my life for the better.

In 1969, huey helicopters were continually taking off and landing from Soc Trang Airfield On this day in 2006, there was no such aerial activity. The rice paddies were gone, replaced by a crush of housing and businesses. I suggested we stop the taxi while I walked over to talk to the guard. Kim said no, that was a bad idea. Maybe she was right that I shouldn't call too much attention to myself. Grudgingly, I settled for shooting photographs of Soc Trang airfield from the rolling taxi and moving on.

Soc Trang had been my home for seven months, a long, long time ago. And somehow, I had managed to come home again, sort of, and say, "Yes, this was the place."

41 - Mayor of Bac Lieu

Cao Trung Kien, former mayor of Bac Lieu, pours a round of drinks. Behind him is a new shopping center that was under construction in Bac Lieu.

Here is the deal: the communists won the Vietnam War, no matter how much we may wish that it were otherwise. They didn't beat the Americans, because we had "Vietnamized" the war and gone home. To be precise, the North Vietnamese beat the South Vietnamese. After the war, the Vietnamese communists expanded their embrace of Marxism-Leninism, and they gloated over their victory. Yet, instead of creating a worker's paradise, they created one of the poorest countries in the world.

In 1979, the Vietnamese had to fight the Chinese, who had been their ally in fighting the United States. The Chinese disapproved of Vietnam's invasion of Cambodia, even though the incursion was at least in part to subdue the murderous Khmer Rouge. This border war made the Vietnamese nervous about the intentions of their much larger neighbor to the north. Then they set out to do what the Vietnamese are really good at: borrow from what works elsewhere. They embraced free trade and sought to rebalance their relationship with the United States. They sought to be the manufacturing engine for developed countries. Not immediately, but surely, slowly. And it worked as the Vietnam economy became one of the fastest growing in Asia.

It was startling at first to find so many items manufactured in Vietnam on American store shelves — everything from clothing and furniture to packaged coconut juice. We witnessed this conversion to free trade first-hand one sunny, hot day, sitting at a table in Bac Lieu in front of a shopping center that was under construction. Our host was the former mayor, Cao Trung Kien, who had been a Viet Cong during the war. More accurately, Mayor Kien and I were sitting at the same table alone for a few minutes without knowing enough of the other's language to carry on a conversation. It was an awkward few moments as we sat and waited for Kim, our translator, to join us at the table. We were relieved when Kim finally sat down and began to translate for us.

In business, networking is important. We were having the first of two meals with Kien because his son was married to one of Kim's nieces. In making small talk, Kien said he would have come over to fight me, if he had known about me in 1969. Yes, he probably would have, although our Bac Lieu communications site was downtown, where the Kitty Kat club — a kind of coffee house and sandwich shop — now sits. We would not have been too hard to find.

197

The truth is that the Viet Cong in the Bac Lieu area were up against one of the best ARVN divisions in Vietnam at that time, and Soc Trang Airfeld was a mighty fortress, against which the Viet Cong could do little other than taking an occasional pot shot. I imagined that Kien had spent a largely underground existence during the war, hiding in swamps and jungles. We both laughed at his comment and shook hands.

Kien was an ex-mayor, but he was still a central figure in leading the province, which had an estimated 800,000 population. He was planning to travel to Minnesota to buy a $7 million water purification system for Bac Lieu. The Swiss had recently completed a pedestrian suspension bridge over the Bac Lieu River, and were planning to build more than two dozen bridges in Bac Lieu province. Kien pointed to an unfinished shopping center. It would be a first for Bac Lieu, which at that time had only the traditional small shops and street vendors. I mentioned to Kien that I was aware of how important education was to the Vietnamese, and all of the college graduates I had met in Kim's family. I related that one day Kim had taken me to visit one of her mother's closest friends. As we stepped into the courtyard house, we saw two teen girls standing there.

"Do you speak English?" I asked.

"Yes, I speak English," one of the girls answered.

"What can you I tell me about Alaska? What do you know about New York? What I can I do improve him improve my English?" she said, peppering me with questions.

"Your English is very good. Keep on practicing," I answered, and tried to fill in a few blanks for her questions about the states. Education was very important to the family. Her mother was a teacher and her father was a retired military pilot.

After a long, friendly conversation, we stood to leave. She tugged at my sleeve and kissed me on the cheek. It was a moving and unexpected gesture. When I relayed this story to the mayor, he nodded and agreed that in many ways education is the key to the future of Vietnam.

Vietnam was experiencing an outbreak of bird flu then. Kien served us duck for lunch, and I silently wondered, "why couldn't it be seafood?" Kien seemed to sense my concern. The duck had been specially inspected to ensure it was disease-free, he said. Someone broke off a piece and dropped it into our bowls. There was no way we were going to insult our host. We picked up our chopsticks and ate some. It was the best duck we ever had. Better yet, there were no ill effects.

42 - Tet

Kim shows her happiness in being reunited with her sisters Hoa, left, and Nga, in Bac Lieu.

Eating good food, drinking beer, and going house to house, socializing with friendly people is my idea of a good time. That was my experience of Tet 2006, the Vietnamese lunar new year celebration. So different than the infamous Tet of 1968, the Year of the Monkey, when the Viet Cong launched their surprise attack all across South Vietnam. I arrived in Vietnam in 1968 a few months after the Viet Cong had been beaten. They were beaten, but the offensive changed minds in America about the war, and soon the drawdown of troops began.

Kim and I had timed our 2006 trip so that we could take part in Tet. It would be the first we spent together in Vietnam since 1971. I had tried to brush up on my Vietnamese, which is negligible to begin with, or as I tell Kim, "I know just enough to be dangerous." Packed in our luggage was a little phrase book titled "Easy Vietnamese." It can be revealed that there is nothing easy about Vietnamese. Using easy and Vietnamese together is is an oxymoron.

The phrase book proved to be largely useless, what with my off-the-mark pronunciation, and the inappropriate phrases:" Dung ban!" (don't shoot) or "Dung co gio tro!" (Don't try any tricks). Going in, I was confident that I could get the gist of any conversation. I was wrong. I was totally dependent on Kim.

Kim and I share a Bac Lieu phone booth in 2006, while she calls family back in the United States.

But being being immersed in Vietnamese for a few weeks, I did learn some new words, including "Kho tin duoc" (that's incredible) and ngon (delicious). When it comes to languages, I may be as dumb as a rock, but I learned that I couldn't go wrong saying "ngon" during mealtime. Not while eating prawn grilled over hot coals, steamed crab, or a seafood and vegetable fondue.

On the main day of Tet, we paid visits to six family homes, and had something to eat at each of them. In addition to all that eating and drinking, Tet is also a time for gift giving, usually money in a little red envelop, and prayers for dead ancestors. Maybe I was out of my element, meeting so many people for the first time, but it was fun, too. I was being invited to light incense at the family altar and say a prayer. I felt honored and unworthy.

Kim's mother's house was filled with family and neighbors the week of Tet. It was so different from American homes, which are often islands of isolation even among neighbors. In America, among my generation, the word "Tet" will always be associated with war. But now I also associate it with strong families and good times.

43 - Chicken and duck

Pausing for a photo in the Great Smokey Mountains.

Chicken and duck.

That's what Kim calls us.

A man and a woman from different races.

From different cultures.

Speaking different languages.

Practicing different religions.

The Buddhist and the Baptist.

Those things matter. They are important.

No, we're not Venus and Mars. It's more like Mercury and Pluto.

Yet, there are similarities. We're both southerners from different countries.

We have similar views on politics, the work ethic, and the family.

We sometimes wonder how it was possible that we met. That we married. That we stayed together. That we stayed in love.

Did it really happen? Or is it just a dream?

Would we do it all again?

I got the better part of the bargain: a smart, tender-hearted beauty, with many talents. I never get tired of seeing her beautiful smile, drawing others to her with her warm personality. In addition to a wife, I got a healer, a cheerleader, a partner, a family banker, and a "naggravator," a combination navigator and and nagger that manifests itself on road trips. Kim can be faint-hearted. She doesn't want to walk up to the edge of a steep mountain and look down, or to ride a roller coaster. But she went places and did things during the Vietnam War that required courage and nerve. She will shoulder any burden for her family, and go beyond the call of duty for everyone else. She has been the instigator for all of our home improvement projects, but also has fearlessly jumped in to help with everything from installing ceramic tile to laying parquet floors, house painting, landscaping and more. Yes, she's a beauty, but she's no delicate princess who worries about her hands and nails.

Kim is a great cook, a woman who thinks creatively in developing new dishes. Favorites include her spicy beef, bun cha gio (Vietnamese noodles served with fried spring rolls and fish sauce), banh xeo (Vietnamese pancake stuffed with fresh vegetables, beansprouts, pork and shrimp), and just about everything else from chili to spaghetti and American pancakes. Ironically, Kim learned how to cook many of her Vietnamese dishes after moving to the United States. Pho and banh xeo are two examples, developed from memory and her own sense of taste.

Penzeys Spices magazine once featured Kim and two of her recipes: sweet and sour pork, and green papaya salad. I didn't marry Kim for her cooking, but I soon discovered that she was skilled in the kitchen and a quick learner.

Aside from" The Spaghetti Incident," with apologies to the band Guns N' Roses. We had hardly settled into our first stateside home when she decided to make spaghetti. Kim has always had a keen sense of taste and smell, and an ability to figure out the ingredients in any dish. Working without a recipe, she can reverse-engineer many entrées. Except in her first attempt at making spaghetti sauce, she fell short. The sauce had just one ingredient: ketchup. She didn't know that while a cook can make his own sauce, it's also available in jars at the local grocery, or in those little packets in the spice aisle.

"Honey, why don't we eat out tonight," I suggested.

Being an Army wife, she borrowed from other cultures, a little German cooking from the frau next door, sushi from a Japanese-Hawaiian couple, Native American-style cornbread from Arizona, cornmeal battered fried shrimp from my mother, and more. Kim developed a reputation over the years as being one of the best supermarket general merchandise

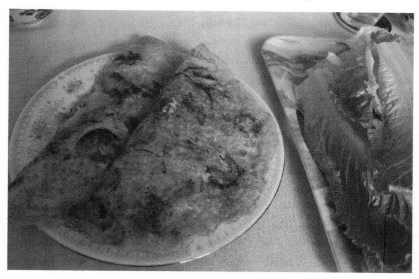

Kim's Banh Xeo.

managers in Florida. She knew the business inside out, was helpful to co-workers and customers alike, and enjoyed the workplace.

Her contributions to the family budget helped create a comfortable standard of living that I couldn't have approached alone. She never hesitated to tell her boss — or me — if something was wrong or needed improving. But she has a talent for doing it in a nice way.

Even when she could hardly afford it, she looked after her family in Vietnam, sending them a few dollars when possible to help with a child's education or a house repair. Kim never stops encouraging and pushing me, and our grown children, and our two grandchildren to do more, be more, and to succeed more. My family was fascinated by some of the folk remedies she brought with her from Vietnam, such as putting a crust of salt on a bruise, using aloe for a skin problem or digestion aid, or pulling a strange weed from the yard for who knows what.

***

Vo duyen!

I savor it like a fine wine when Kim says "vo duyen." She says it full of indignation and humor. In her southern Vietnamese dialect, it sounds like

In Saigon, a few weeks before the move to the United States.

"yo yeen." It might sound like she is calling me a name. But she is not. It essentially means, "that's not nice," or "that's not appropriate." Linguists will disagree with my interpretation. If so, understand that I know just enough Vietnamese to be dangerous.

Kim is not a name caller.

But she will call me out.

"You get angry too easy."

"You have no patience."

"You don't walk, you hop, like when you were in the Army."

"You don't chew your food. You swallow it whole. Slow down."

Sometimes she reflects on her life with a "vo duyen."

"You are a romantic. Why are you always trying to hold my hand?"

206

"You have changed a lot from when we first met. You were handsome, and slim. Look at you now."

"I still wonder why you wanted to marry me. Do you still love me?"

'When I first met you, you were very quiet. Now you talk all the time, make jokes, and sing in the car."

True. I do sing in the car. Badly.

***

Kim gives me her classic 'vo duyen' look.

Sometimes Kim will reflect back on her childhood.

"It wasn't so hard," she will say. "It was the life we knew I worked in the rice field. I didn't know any other way."

When life got really tough at home and her parents had a hard time feeding all their children, they would send her to live with an aunt, who treated her like her own daughter. "She was my favorite aunt," Kim says.

No wonder.

I introduced Kim to pizza in 1971 at Long Binh, Vietnam. She refused to eat it. "It looked disgusting," she said. I can see how someone who had never before seen a pizza could have such an opinion.

Much has changed since the Vietnam War, both in the United States and in Vietnam. In 2017, Kim returned to Vietnam with several of her girlfriends. While in Vietnam, Kim took her nephews and nieces out for a treat and asked them what they wanted. "Pizza," they said.

She had to laugh. The world had turned upside down.

44— New millennium

On the mend at Blake Medical Center after three hours of surgery. Photo by Christine D. Jones

Funny thing about recovering from anesthesia: you just wake up when the operation is over, assuming everything went well. At least that's how it seemed to this patient. Of course, there is more to it than that, including how well the anesthesiology team and the surgeon did their work. I regained consciousness in my room at Bradenton's Blake Medical Center after a three-hour operation on May 23, 2018, and saw Kim, who was holding my hand, and our daughter Christine. I smiled and said hello to them. It was a beautiful sight, seeing the concern lift from their faces.

"I love you two," I said.

Dr. Paul Toomey had performed robot surgery through four small incisions in my abdomen. The procedure was a right hemicolectomy. Removal of my right large intestine. The surgery was necessary to remove a polyp that refused to be lifted during a colonoscopy. I needed no persuading to have this precautionary surgery. My grandmother died from colorectal cancer, and my mother died after having surgery for an intestinal blockage. Fortunately for me, I went into the surgery with a strong constitution, and good health. I am lucky that way because neither my father nor my mother were as healthy as me at the same age. Being a lifelong nonsmoker and runner helps.

Kim plants a kiss on my growing forehead at Blake Medical Center. Photo by Christine D. Jones

Neither Kim nor Christine had ever seen me afflicted with anything worse than a cold. This was different, potentially life threatening. Over the next three days, Kim and Christine spent endless hours with me, as I began my recovery. Our son Dan, in California, was concerned, too, and checked in frequently by phone.

As close as we are, I was nevertheless moved by their devotion and caring. This is what family is really all about, I thought. Families are by nature dysfunctional, but when it counts, everyone pulls together.

"Dad, you didn't know this, but your surgery was traumatic for Mom," Christine said. "She cried when you weren't looking."

"Well, what did you say to reassure her everything would be OK?" I asked.

"I told her, 'Gee, Mom, it's not like he had a baby or something,'" Christine said.

That's my girl.

Going into the surgery, my 87-year-old aunt Verona prayed with me over the phone. It was such a powerful spiritual experience that I felt my hair standing on end. It was that electrifying. All of that, and the care and encouragement of the nurses at Blake, who treated me like a rock star each time I achieved a new milestone, made for a speedy recovery. Not to say that turning on my side initially wasn't painful, or that a little cough wouldn't be a terrifying adventure as I grabbed a pillow and held it tightly to my abdomen.

But otherwise, there was no pain. A Tylenol drip kept me comfortable, and I never needed a stronger painkiller. Coincidentally, Aunt Verona and I were in different hospitals at the same time. She was having a procedure for her heart. We checked on each other during our stays via text message. The only unpleasant part of my hospital stay was the nasogastric intubation device that a nurse ran up my nose to my stomach after I threw up my first night in the hospital. The tube was to suction any remaining contents from my stomach. Removal of that tube a day later was an instant morale boost.

After three nights in the hospital, I went home and quickly began getting back to normal. It was progress to be able to easily get out of bed, or to cough without grabbing my abdomen in pain. Finally, I got the word that the pathology from my intestine was benign. I received a clean bill of health. In just a matter of weeks, I was eating whatever I wanted, driving, and back in the newsroom, writing stories.

God is good. God is always good. The ability of the human body to heal is miraculous. There is a Higher Power.

Reading about someone's colonoscopy and his right hemicolectomy may seem like too much information for some. Consider it a public service announcement. Get your annual physical. Get that colonoscopy.

***

Baby boomers have been called one of the most self-centered, selfish, spoiled generations ever. But as we moved into the new millennium, time and history proved that it was never all about us. Time and history move on with us or without us.

The Vietnam War might have been the major event of our lives, but the terrorist attacks of 9/11 and the Great Recession were coming. We never figured it all out or made it a better world.

Not the bomb-throwing weathermen, the hippies, or the silent majority.

Hatred, greed, intolerance, lust, and envy are still with us. As are war, pestilence, disease, poverty, and economic upheaval.

Flower power wasn't the answer. Neither was yuppie greed on Wall Street.

Those who made the most sense were those in the middle who got honest jobs, raised families, sought to do good in their church and community.

Technology was the genie in the bottle that changed a lot of equations.

Medicine — did I mention robot surgery? — social media, and home computers have been prime movers.

Who doesn't yearn for simpler days, when the problems seemed so much more manageable?

Go to the moon? Win World War II? Cure polio? Well, OK then!

The changing times followed me into the newsroom, too, where new technology wiped out composing rooms, typesetting operations, copy desks, and pre-press areas.

New computers allowed management to continually shrink newsroom staffs.

Early in my career, it was frowned upon for reporters to shoot their own photos. Now, anyone fortunate enough to still be writing probably shoots their own photos and produces videos as well. Not only that, but they had darned well better be sure to write something that people want to read online. I have no complaints about any of that. I am the fortunate dinosaur lucky enough to still have a job, and to be able to write about news that matters to the community. It remains fun, and I enjoy the interaction with the public, and the opportunity to learn something new.

And I enjoy working with young reporters. It amazes me how hard they work, how smart they are, and how dedicated they are in reporting the news for our readers. They do it for little money, with honesty, and with plenty of guts at a time when everyone in the business is smeared with the same "fake-news" brush.

No, at this point I am in overtime in my career, and if it all ended today, I would say the last few years have been pure gravy.

***

Technology. No, I don't hate it.

I love to see Kim on her iPhone or her iPad, communicating by Facetime or messenger with her family in Vietnam, or texting one of her buddies, or a grandchild, complete with emojis.

But my, what I would really like to see is someone invent a time machine.

The places I would go, and the folks I would see.

45 - Echoes

We couldn't stop smiling on Dec 14, 1970, during our wedding in the chapel at Long Binh, Vietnam. We still can't.

For any Vietnam veteran there are two journeys he or she will never forget. One is to visit the Vietnam Memorial in Washington, D.C., which pays tribute to those who lost their lives, and all their tomorrows in Vietnam. Walking into the Memorial, which seems to be cut into the earth, and seeing more than 58,000 names brings tears to the eyes. Has any memorial ever been more emotionally charged in its simplicity?

The other journey is a return visit to Vietnam to see the country at peace.

The most moving part of my return visit to Vietnam was getting to know my wife's family. I felt love and respect from those generous, wonderful people. Wherever we went, we received smiles and a sincere welcome. Even at a roadside barbershop, we were offered cigarettes and coffee before getting a haircut. I found myself falling in love with my wife's family. I found that I cared very much about what happens to them. I told Kim how much I enjoyed the trip and how much affection I felt for her family. I had to ask her, what did they think about me, the big-nosed, hairy foreigner?

"Why, they loved you," Kim said.

***

Margie Jones, my stepmother, became the keeper of the flame for Jimmy Jones Hot Sauce, and other family memories. Even after she, too, left St. Augustine and moved near West Palm Beach to live the rest of her life with my sister Kathy and her husband Chuck.

In 2011, at a surprise 80th birthday party for Margie, my sister Nancy who had been making the sauce on and off for years, brought each of us a freshly made batch with original Jimmy Jones Hot Sauce labels that had been printed more than 25 years earlier.

The new batch of sauce touched off a wave of remembrance and nostalgia. My daughter Christine who tasted the Jimmy Jones hot sauce when she was a little girl recently asked for a copy of the recipe and made a batch of her own.

When Margie passed away in 2014, all six of her surviving children and stepchildren attended the funeral, in a display of affection that might have seemed improbable at the merging of two families back in 1959.

Throughout my Army travels, Margie was one of my most faithful letter writers. She even fixed me up with a date while I was home on leave between Germany and Vietnam. When Kim and I finally came to the United States together in 1971, Margie embraced her new daughter-in-law. Margie admitted to Kim one time that if she had it to do over again as a stepmother she might have done things differently. It's hard being a stepmother, just as it can be hard being a stepchild. Margie was a very bright woman, who had progressive ideas about what is right and wrong in society.

215

She had a wry sense of humor and a ready laugh, even though she had her share of hard knocks in life. In high school, she sat out a year to take care of her mother who was dying of cancer. She also cared for my dad during his illness with ALS and called to say that he was sinking fast and we should come to say our farewells. She was with him when he passed away one night at home. Even though I didn't see a lot of Margie after she moved to Palm Beach County, we stayed in touch. She called me "son" or "Jimmy."

We would talk about Gator football, or I would joke with her that we should go out dancing, drink some whiskey, and smoke a cigar. Unfortunately, we never did.

***

It was late on an August afternoon. I was working on a newspaper story. I wanted to know what neighbors thought of a developer's plan to build 500 homes next door to them. I saw a fellow sitting in his open garage, smoking a cigar. I stopped and introduced myself. He said his name was Ray. A little bit apologetically, Ray said that he was working on his fourth beer.

"Sounds like the traffic I escaped in New Jersey 25 years ago is coming to my neighborhood," he said.

It had nothing to do with the story, but when I spotted a Vietnam Service Medal decal on his pickup truck, I had to ask him about it. He told me he was an Army veteran and had arrived in Vietnam in March 1968, serving there for 28 months. He was in I Corps, the military region closest to the demilitarized zone. Places like Dong Ha, Phu Bai and Quang Tri.

Later, he had been a driver for generals in the Long Binh area. I asked why he has spent so much time in Vietnam. He looked around to see if his wife was in earshot.

"I had a Vietnamese girlfriend," Ray said. "I planned to marry her, but I ran out of time."

I understand, I answered, explaining that I had my own struggle to marry my sweetheart.

216

Later I thought about our conversation and wondered how many other G.I.s might have had Vietnamese girlfriends and still wonder about them all these years later. Where is the woman they loved? Is she still alive? What might have been?

I don't have to wonder about what might have been.

I found a woman I could love and better yet who loved me back.

Life hasn't always been easy.

Fortunately, love can grow, mature, deepen. We raised two children who are bright, strong, responsible adults. We are proud of them for their decency, their caring, and their sense of family.

Kim is right here with me. Maybe she's tending her orchids, or in the kitchen, rattling pots and pans, or visiting with one of her many friends.

Whatever Kim is doing, I know that she loves me and her family.

No, I have never had to be sorry. I am the lucky one.

Made in the USA
Columbia, SC
13 July 2020